Motown

Celebrating 60 Years Of Amazing Music

Pete McKenna

NEW HAVEN PUBLISHING LTD

Published 2020
NEW HAVEN PUBLISHING LTD
www.newhavenpublishingltd.com
newhavenpublishing@gmail.com

Cover design © Pete Cunliffe
pcunliffe@blueyonder.co.uk

Front and back cover images
@Al Abrams, Motown Black and White Collection

newhaven
publishing

ISBN: 978-1-912587-35-3

A big thank you to Teddie and the team at New Haven Publishing for making this happen – to my Carmen Del Castillo for keeping me going through thick and thin and to Ged Grennell and Glenn Walker Foster for their invaluable friendship.

Content

FOREWORD
by
GLENN WALKER FOSTER

Firstly I would like to say a few words about the author Pete "Chess" McKenna, who I've known since late 1974. On more than one occasion he has put pen to paper describing life growing up as a teenager in the 70s when skinheads and suedeheads were prominent, followed by the soul boys who developed an obsession with and love of rare soul music which was eventually tagged "northern soul" - an obsession and love Pete and myself shared vehemently, creating a bond which keeps us friends over forty years later, as strong as it ever was. I'm sure that, without question, Tamla Motown both initiated and hugely influenced our soulful odyssey.

And now to Tamla Motown itself, possibly THE most successful record label in our lifetime, generated from Hitsville USA Detroit in 1959. Their first label was called simply Tamla, with their first record being Tamla 101 - 'Come to Me' by Marv Johnson. The label was split into four different names - Tamla, Gordy, Soul and Tamla UK which was specifically aimed at the growing UK market, but there were other labels to come that fell under the Motown umbrella.

Luckily at the time I'd been one of the DJs at our "school discos" and various youth clubs in Blackpool and

Lytham St Annes and Motown music became critical to our playlists. Many coffee bars up and down the Fylde Coast had jukeboxes which were full of Motown singles, which were played more than any other music genre. If I had just a pound for all the times I listened to 'What Becomes of the Brokenhearted?' by Jimmy Ruffin on a jukebox I would be a very rich man. Solely for this reason it still remains a stand out sound for me. For a teenager living in 70s UK having been drip fed on the chart music of the day, Tamla Motown was such a refreshing joy to the ears. That simple but effective solid four four beat, with songs full of heartfelt lyrics about falling in and out of love being the dominant theme, was something most people could easily relate to.

I was and still am a massive Rolling Stones fan; their R and B based music instantly struck a chord inside me and in the early 70s I listened to little else but my favourite song 'Can I Get A Witness'. Of course eventually the inevitable happened as a boy a couple of years older than me asked: "Hey, Glenn mate. Have you heard the Marvin Gaye version?" offering to lend me the single to take home and listen to, which of course I did. It was fabulous and from that important moment in time in my life I began collecting Tamla Motown records. I remember all too well that school dinner tickets were selling for sixty pence a time so in my final year I made my mind up to sell as many as I could to all the fat boys knowing that eventually, come the end of the week, I'd walk from school to the coin shop on Bond Street – later renamed Melody Records – and buy myself five Tamla Motown singles.

Eunice, the lady who owned the shop, was so thoroughly intrigued by my dinner ticket story that she kindly used to give me six singles for the price of five. My collection of Motown singles quickly began to swell with some like Stevie Wonder's classic 'Superstition' and 'Living for the City' amongst my favourites, along with

'Keep on Trucking' by Eddie Kendricks rarely off my turntables at home. One record in particular that was different from the rest was a haunting unusual Motown offering called 'Child of Love' by Caston and Majors, along with a rare reggae offering 'Young Gifted and Black' by Bob and Marcia I still play today. Another one hugely popular to me was and still is the driving beat of R Dean Taylor's 'Ghost In My House'. He was one of the rare white artists to record for Motown and it was a single that was a massive hit on the northern soul scene.

Back to the jukebox and once again stand out popular singles by many of the girls on the scene who were rapidly falling under the magical Motown spell were of course 'Baby Love', 'Where Did Our Love Go' and 'Stop In The Name Of Love' courtesy of The Supremes, along with hits from The Four Tops like 'Reach Out I'll Be There'. I mean who wasn't mesmerised by the incredible vocal range of their lead singer Levi Stubbs? And then there was The Temptations with singles like 'Take A Look Around' and the one and only Martha Reeves with classic hits like 'Dancing In The Street'.

I found it interesting that singles from Motown's golden years of '65 and '66 together with their prolific output were adored by British youth as our passion for rare soul music grew. The one and only Edwin Starr established himself as one of Motown's truly great artists with singles like 'Backstreet', '25 Miles', 'Agent OO Soul' and 'I Have Faith In You' along with other popular dancefloor fillers like 'It Takes Two' by Marvin Gaye and Kim Weston and the storming one hundred miles an hour 'Tell Me It's Just A Rumour' by the Isley Brothers.

I could talk about so many countless other successful singles on various labels that Motown recorded but that would indeed be a book in itself. Suffice to say that the unique infectious sound of young America totally captivated a generation who still to this day continue to listen to those records with as much affection as they did when they were newly released; which leads me nicely on to the 60th celebration of Tamla Motown, so without further ado, I will now hand you over to the author of this story. As my final word on the subject, I will leave you with my personal all-time favourite Tamla Motown track 'I'm Just A Mortal Man' by the one and only Jimmy Ruffin and a massive thank you to our own gorgeous queen of soul Dusty Springfield for all her talent and endless hard work in popularising the sound of Tamla Motown.

Glenn Walker Foster

INTRODUCTION

This year, 2020, celebrates the 60th anniversary of arguably the most successful American recording label, which changed the sound and face of black American soul music forever - leaving me begging the question: "Where have all the years gone?" In 1960, during troubled times when racial tensions were simmering to murdering point, making normal daily life for black Americans difficult and often dangerous to say the least, imbued with an unshakeable vision, a determined self-belief and a remarkable instinct for spotting latent talent in the making, the young Berry Gordy pulled off the seemingly impossible by acquiring a modest building in Detroit which was destined to become the headquarters of Tamla Motown records. He christened it Hitsville USA, and, as they say, the rest is history.

In a cramped recording studio, aided and abetted by the legendary Tamla Motown in-house band the Funk Brothers, who played on almost every Motown track recorded, the superstars of the future were born; and the list is impressive to say the least. Diana Ross and the Supremes – Martha Reeves and the Vandellas – Stevie Wonder – Marvin Gaye – Smokey Robinson and the Miracles – the Four Tops – the Temptations – the Elgins – the Isley

Brothers – Jackie Wilson – R Dean Taylor – Brenda Holloway – Chuck Jackson – Jimmy Ruffin – Edwin Starr – Tammi Terrell – Earl Van Dyke – Kim Weston – Frankie Valli – Mary Wells – the Jacksons - the list goes on and on; and what a list.

Berry Gordy originally created Tamla records on Jan 12th 1959, specifically for the UK market. Many diehard soul fans even today feel that was his best ever label. The name was inspired by the 1957 film *Tammy and the Batchelor* about an ordinary young woman from Mississippi who falls in love with Southern gentleman. The film was a big favourite of Gordy's and featured the song 'Tammy' sung by Debby Reynolds, which provided the inspiration behind his decision to create the label which boasted many of the soon to be famous stars. He renamed it Tamla Motown on April 14th 1960, the name paying homage to Motor City, Detroit, the city Gordy felt at home in. The first UK release was 'Stop In The Name Of Love' by the Supremes in May 1965, followed by over forty more singles in the same year. It was an incredible output earning Tamla Motown the nickname "the factory" due to it remaining open for business over twenty hours a day. This allowed busy touring artists to drop in, record a couple of songs and pick up on the tour again when the recording session was over.

They were the new soul ambassadors, spreading the unique Motown sound to the world desperate for the new sound, and influencing British artists like the Foundations and Dusty Springfield. As the Tamla Motown sound became more popular, artists from all over the world flocked to the Hitsville studio in Detroit like lemmings, hoping to capture some of that magical sound in their own music. They wrongly assumed that it was the city of Detroit itself that was solely responsible for creating the sound; but how wrong they were, as Smokey Robinson clearly dispelled the myth in this early quote.

"When we were first successful with it, people were coming from Germany, France, Italy, Alabama, New York, California. From everywhere just to record in Detroit. They figured it was in the air that if they came to Detroit and recorded, they'd get the Motown sound. The Motown sound to me is not an audible sound. It's spiritual, it comes from the people that make it happen. What people didn't realise is that we just had one studio there but we recorded in Chicago, Nashville, New York, almost every big city and we still got the Motown sound."

Right from the beginning Gordy's mission was to produce danceable, infectious, instantly recognisable commercial black American soul music, and this he did brilliantly. Much of the music echoed personal adolescent experiences all teenagers went through: boy and girl meet - boy and girl fall in love - boy and girl split up - and boy and girl get back together again - or not. People could see themselves in the lyrics and they loved them. It was a tried and tested recipe for success without the need to change a thing up until the Detroit riots in 1967.

For many of us who grew up in 60s and 70s Britain, 2020 marks a very special year in the music calendar, it being the sixtieth anniversary of the truly legendary Tamla Motown records. How can any of us who were into the Tamla soul scene back then forget those brilliant times when we were young and carefree and the impossible was anything but, unable to resist the pull of the dance floor when a particular favourite record burst into life? Songs recorded by great artists that have remained in us ever since like DNA infused in our bones. Songs played as we kissed and cuddled our future partners - eighteenth and twenty-first birthday parties - engagements, marriages and funerals, saying our final farewells to cherished loved ones and friends, watching them slowly disappear behind the damson coloured velvet curtain.

Ever since the First World War, the United States of America and the United Kingdom have shared a strong unbeatable alliance in times of war but in the 60s and 70s, an alliance of an entirely different nature took place: an invasion of the new stateside imported soul music to satisfy the needs of British soul fans, desperate to hear the new soul sounds. It was a music that fit in perfectly with our lifestyles, comprising sharp suits and casual clothes, cash in our pockets, all leather shoes, Lambretta and Vespa scooters, weekend nightclubs, amphetamines, chatting up girls and occasional violence if absolutely necessary.

Stateside recording labels like Chess, Stax, Atlantic and Motown provided us with a staple diet of soul music that boasted many great soul artists, some of which went on to fame and fortune while others fell by the wayside. Chess records was a highly respected label formed in Chicago in 1950 by the unlikely partnership of Leonard and Phil Chess, two Jewish immigrants from Poland whose musical tastes ranged from gospel, blues, rhythm and blues, soul, jazz and rock. Chess records signed many famous artists of the day including Chuck Berry, Muddy Waters, the Flamingos, Howlin Wolf, John Lee Hooker, Sonny Stitt, Memphis Slim, Johnny Guitar Watson, Sonny Boy Williamson and Buddy Guy to name but a few.

Stax was originally called Satellite records until it was renamed four years later, in 1961. It was based in Memphis Tennessee and created by the brother and sister team of Jim Stewart and Estella Acton. With racial tensions and violence boiling over at the time, Stax managed to keep everything they recorded in house. With cash a little thin on the ground, they got by using one recording studio, one set of equipment and a group of musicians they used all the time. This lack of facilities was later recognised as being the catalyst for the creation of the unique Stax musical sound, steeped in the history of the blues, country, gospel and rhythm and blues, and from 1957 to 1975, their signed artists were legendary, including Booker T and the MG's, Rufus Thomas, Otis Redding, Carla Thomas, Sam and Dave, Eddie Floyd, Johnny Taylor, Kim Weston, William Bell, The Bar Kays, Isaac Hayes, Little Milton, the Staple Singers, Ruby Johnson and many more.

One of the driving forces behind the creation of Atlantic records came in the unlikely form of Ahmet Ertegan, a Turkish philanthropist and passionate music lover born into a wealthy aristocratic family. After deciding to follow his dream, he moved to America to become the co-founder of Atlantic records with his partner Herb Abramson, who hailed from a Jewish family in Brooklyn. His strong passion for music put paid to a lucrative career in dentistry, and along with Ertegan he created Atlantic records in 1947, signing many legendary artists like Archie Bell and the Drells, Lavern Baker, Maggie Bell, Clarence Carter, Ray Charles, The Coasters, John Coltrane, the Drifters, Roberta Flack, Aretha Franklin, Major Harris, Ben E King, Alexis Korner, Joe Tex the Trammps, Mary Wells, Betty Wright and the late great Otis Redding, who sadly passed away years before his time.

Between them, Chess, Stax and Atlantic undoubtably produced some fantastic music, but for me they lacked that all important "stop what you're doing right now and listen to that record" effect that Tamla Motown had on me ever since the first time I heard '25 Miles' by the legendary Edwin Starr back in 1968. It was a storming track performed by one of Motown's giants of soul which instantly brightened up a boring Thursday night mathematics homework session. And so, at the tender age of thirteen, my love affair with Tamla Motown began. The following Saturday morning I dashed up to spend some of my pocket money on my first ever Motown single, '25 Miles', from what was the best record shop in Blackpool.

Sinfonia Records on Cookson Street was owned by the one and only Sandy Mountain, a good living, devout Christian whose vast musical knowledge was the equivalent of a joint Oxford Cambridge degree, always ready and willing to advise a customer trying to track down a particular single or LP. A Saturday morning ritual rapidly developed for me: a visit to Sandy's empire before a cappuccino coffee and a bacon toastie in the Beehive, me the raw soul apprentice rubbing shoulders with the older cooler soul boys. Their gleaming customised Lambrettas and Vespas were parked up with military precision outside the shop and they were all dressed in sheepskins, Ben Sherman's, Fred Perry's, Levi jeans and cherry red Doc Martens. Some three years later, having served my soul apprenticeship, I became one of the older respected soul boys myself, rubbing shoulders with the young lads asking Sandy for some advice about a record they'd heard.

Along with the mass of singles flooding the UK, Motown also produced a fantastic series of LPs called Motown Chartbusters, releasing twelve LPs between 1967 and 1982. All twelve made the top UK charts, making them the most successful selling series of LPs until the mid-1980s. For around three pounds you got an LP with brilliant artwork on the cover featuring around fifteen tracks recorded by the very best Motown artists: Stevie Wonder – the Supremes – the Four Tops – the Temptations – Edwin Starr – Jimmy Ruffin – Junior Walker – the Contours – Martha Reeves and the Vandellas – Gladys Knight – Marvin Gaye and Tammi Terrell – Smokey Robinson and the Miracles – Marv Johnson - the Isley Brothers – R Dean Taylor – Kim Weston – Brenda Holloway – Barbara McNair - Chuck Jackson – the Marvelettes – Earl Van Dyke – Thelma Houston and more providing the best quality for money LPs ever produced.

At the grand old age of ninety, Berry Gordy's wealth since he created Tamla Motown is reputed to be three hundred and forty-five million dollars, although some say it's closer to the four hundred million mark. Without doubt he has packed a lot into his life as a songwriter, record executive, television and film producer, and he still is the highest earning African American businessman. Compared to today's multi billionaires and footballers, though, Gordy's fortune is a mere drop in the ocean; compared, for example, to the likes of Roman Abramovic whose estimated fortune totals over a staggering twelve billion dollars and rising and who is also number nine in the top twenty list of billionaire football club owners.

That's all good and well but in my opinion, what makes Gordy's route to fame and fortune both so impossible and incredible is the fact that he started out in Detroit in 1959 with only eight hundred dollars to his name. He was a determined black visionary with a dream to create what eventually turned out to be the most successful African American record label in a country that was still heavily racist - Berry Gordy wasn't going to allow that to get in his way to fame and fortune.

Even as early as the sixties, Motown's meteoric success was staggering. Here was a record label boasting eight more, each with their own management service. Gordy's own publishing company was earning him millions of dollars each year and the success just kept coming, like he was a man who could do no wrong. In the three years between 1964 and '67 Motown scored an incredible fourteen number one pop singles, twenty number one R and B chart singles, forty-six more top fifteen singles plus seventy-five other top fifteen R and B chart singles. In 1966 a staggering seventy-five percent of Motown releases featured in the charts, an achievement which earned Hitsville the nickname The Factory. This was all more than enough proof that he'd pulled off the impossible, but there was so much more to come before the final episode starring Berry Gordy and Tamla Motown had played out.

Pete McKenna

ROOTS

This story coincides with the celebration of the sixtieth birthday of Tamla Motown, a milestone for the man who made it all possible, Berry Gordy. Just one music genre in the rich, diverse, hugely influential tapestry of black American music around the world, taking its place alongside gospel, blues, rhythm and blues, jazz, soul, funk, disco, early house, garage, and rap. I mean, think about our personal record collections for a second. Take away all the vinyl and compact discs that we've amassed over the years that haven't been influenced by black music in some form or another and what would we have left apart from Chas and Dave's greatest hits or England's World Cup anthems? And this black music was born out of the constant pain and abuse suffered by black African slaves forced to spend their lives working for nothing on the plantations in the American Confederacy; which fittingly enough is where this story has to begin, because without that terrible heritage, black music would not be the powerful force it is today.

The first slaves arrived in America as early as 1619 on board a ship called The White Lion, which delivered twenty scared, bewildered people to the British owned colony of Jamestown in Virginia. The second truly terrifying ordeal slaves faced, after being beaten and dragged from their villages, was life on the slave ships: after a cursory medical they were herded downstairs into the hold, a dark, hellish world where they were chained and stacked together with barely enough room to move for up to two to three months, often lying on their sides for the duration of the journey, resembling something like a huge human bookcase.

For many of the slaves, life became so unbearable that they jumped overboard, but in time, due to special nets fitted on the ships, this was no longer an option. Naturally disease was rife under such inhuman conditions, the two main killer diseases being dysentery and smallpox. Slaves were looked on as nothing more than commercial cargo and could be sacrificed for the greater good of the voyage. One such terrible incident occurred on the slave ship Zong in November 1871. With the crew desperately low on water and supplies, the captain gave the order to unchain one hundred and fifty slaves, including women and children, and throw them overboard.

If the slaves survived the journey, they were put to work in the plantations. By 1860 the slave population in America had grown to over four million. They were forced to endure truly miserable, indescribable lives, without basic human rights, beaten and restricted in just about every way imaginable. Even the drums that they had been brought up listening to from early childhood were banned, for fear of them being used to communicate with slaves in other plantations to plan a rebellion. That said, the power of song was widely used by the slaves working in the cotton fields to help to get them through another backbreaking, hopeless day.

Eventually some two hundred and forty years of slavery came to an end when Abraham Lincoln announced the abolition of such an inhuman practice, but the South vehemently rejected any such change to the centuries-old life they enjoyed and took for granted. With the two sides bitterly opposed the American Civil War began. Fought between 1861 and 1865, it was the worst conflict in American history, with conservative estimates claiming that over 620,000 soldiers were killed in battle with many more thousands suffering truly appalling injuries.

The war to end slavery was a bloody victory for Abraham Lincoln and the North, but for the now free African Americans, things were about to get unexpectedly worse. Wild white lynch mobs went on the rampage through a number of the Southern states, torturing and killing former slaves for no other reason than their colour. 'Strange Fruit' was originally a poem written by Abe Meeropol in 1937 which tells the grim story of what remains of African Americans after a typical lynching. Two years later Billie Holliday recorded a haunting song based on the poem, describing in graphic detail black people hanging from trees, which was a commonplace sight in the South. Those terrible images of man's extreme inhumanity to man eventually became an important focal point for the Civil Rights Movement as it gained momentum across America. Billie Holliday's song was voted the best song of the century by *Time* magazine in 1999 and the *New Statesman* called it one of the all-time top twenty political protest songs. Ironically enough, the *Atlanta Journal*, the place where so many lynchings occurred, listed it number one in the one hundred songs of the South.

Even after the abolition of slavery, the treatment of many African Americans was still nothing short of inhuman. Segregation was an everyday way of life for the majority of black people in many Southern states due to a series of ludicrous laws called the "Jim Crow" laws. The name came from a white actor called Thomas "Daddy" Rice who created the fictional character of a black minstrel former slave called Jim Crow, who was dim-witted, stupid and clumsy. The audiences loved the act. The Jim Crow laws enforced segregation in virtually all facets of daily public life. Intermarriage between blacks and whites was banned; blacks were banned from playing baseball; businesses were forced to keep their black and white clients strictly separated, with separate dining in restaurants, and employers even had to provide separate toilet facilities for black and white employees; buses and trains had to provide separate seating, waiting rooms and ticket windows for blacks and whites; blind blacks had to be cared for in separate facilities; dead blacks were prohibited from being buried next to a white grave; hospitals were forced to provide separate entrances and treatment areas for blacks and whites; whites renting property to blacks could be fined up to one hundred dollars and imprisoned for up to sixty days; all theatres and cinemas were forced to separate black and white audiences - the list of restrictions goes on and on.

Life for African Americans was both appalling and dangerous back in the 1950s and 60s. Something had to give to improve their situation and it did thanks to the actions of one brave woman who was sick and tired of being treated as a less than second class citizen. The woman in question was Rosa Parks, who lived in Montgomery, and she risked her life by having the courage when she was on board a bus to refuse to give her seat up to a white person. By automatically breaking the segregation laws, Rosa was arrested and held for trial. Many people claim that this incident provided the catalyst for the birth of the Civil Rights Movement.

As the news quickly spread across the country, the African American population fought back by organising a year-long boycott of the bus system, causing such a furore that the case actually made it to the Supreme Court, which ruled that the bus companies desegregate the system. Thus the Civil Rights Movement was born, attracting peace activists like Martin Luther King, Fred Shuttleworth and

Charlie Steele, who along with many others moulded the movement into a powerful force, undertaking decades of work before the positions of African Americans improved.

Increasing numbers of men and women were inspired by the actions of Rosa Parks in bravely going where many blacks feared to tread for obvious reasons. They entered shops, cafes, bars, restaurants, cinemas and theatres taking their rightful places to sit with the white people. They were met with strong resentment, tension and violence on a large scale, and in places like Birmingham and Montgomery full scale riots broke out between blacks and white racists backed up by the equally racist police, army and National Guard, who viciously beat any black men and women who dared stand in their way before turning the water cannons on them.

The tremors of this increasing social unrest were felt in the White House as the biggest political march in American history arrived in Washington. Over two hundred and fifty thousand people gathered - eighty percent of them black people - who listened to one of the greatest speeches in history, delivered by Martin Luther King, who "had a dream," that began a year later with the passing of the Civil Rights Act 1964. The same year as the people marched on the White House, President John F Kennedy was assassinated by persons unknown in Dallas followed by Malcolm X in 1965 and Dr Martin Luther King in 1968. The Civil Rights Movement was dealt a massive blow but it became stronger and more focussed on the fight for equality.

Malcolm X was the outspoken and controversial Muslim activist and minister leader of the Nation of Islam, whose teachings heavily influenced two young passionate black men, Bobby Seale and Huey Newton, who founded the Black Panthers, indirectly part of the Civil Rights Movement but favouring more militant, aggressive action. They wore uniform style clothing, black berets and black leather jackets, but with around only two thousand members, they were in reality completely ineffective against the might of America's intelligence agencies, who had them under constant surveillance from day one. Their main roles were policing neighbourhoods and harassing police patrols in several cities across America, unfortunately attracting a number of criminals who operated for their own good under the Black Panthers banner. They were involved in numerous gun battles with the police resulting in Huey Newton being arrested and jailed for fifteen years for allegedly shooting a policeman to death, the sentence eventually being overturned by the court of appeal.

The Panthers saw themselves as soldiers at the forefront of the fight for black equality but their policy of armed self-defence prompted the FBI head J Edgar Hoover to call them "the greatest threat to national security." Constant pressure from security forces coupled with bitter internal arguments sealed the end of the Black Panthers in 1982 but many even today think their agenda is more relevant than ever. Fred Hampton, another hugely influential member of the Black Panthers, who was killed by police, left oppressed people the world over with the following message: "We don't think you should fight fire with fire – we think you should fight it with water – we're going to fight racism not with racism but with solidarity – we say we're not going to fight capitalism with black capitalism but with socialism – we're going to fight their reactions with all us people getting together and having an international proletarian revolution."

In 1968, during the medal ceremony in the Olympic stadium in Mexico, two African American athletes called Tommie Smith and John Carlos introduced the world to Black Power. After they were awarded their gold and bronze medals, they raised an arm, each wearing black gloves, as a salute to their brothers' and sisters' struggles. The remaining athlete and silver medallist Peter Norman joined the protest by wearing the Olympic Project for Human Rights badge. The Olympic Committee expelled Smith and Carlos from the games for daring to bring politics into the sporting arena, prompting Tommie Smith to make the following statement that summed up the struggle of every African American: "If I win I'm an American, not a black American, but if I did something bad then they would say I'm a Negro. We are black and we are proud of being black. Black America will understand what we did tonight."

BERRY GORDY CREATED MOTOWN

All legends have to begin somewhere and essentially Tamla Motown began somewhat prematurely on the 28th November 1929 with the birth of Berry Gordy. He would become the man who would eventually turn Tamla Motown into one of the biggest, most successful American recording labels in music history. His parents were Berry Gordy Senior and Bertha Fuller Gordy, baby Berry being the seventh of eight children: Fuller, Esther, Anna, Loucye, George, Gwen, Berry and Robert.

The Gordy family were far removed from the typical black American family at the time. They were wealthy middle class business people, owning a successful painting and construction company, and Bertha went on to co-found a successful insurance company called the Mutual Life. It was a far cry from how Berry's grandfather, Berry Gordy the first, began his life as the son of a wealthy southern plantation owner called James Gordy, while Berry's half-brother became former president Jimmy Carter's grandfather.

At that time in stateside social history, Detroit Michigan was a hugely successful city, being the centre of the mighty American automobile manufacturing industry with Ford, Packard, Hudson, Studebaker, Chrysler and Lincoln Mercury all based there, in massive factories, offering plenty of well paid jobs to all and sundry. They were factories in which a number of future Motown stars sang their days away on the production lines, hoping for the break of a lifetime. The work was long and hard but the wages were above average, offering black Americans a chance to live their lives on an equal basis with their white co-workers.

This was just one of the reasons why the young Berry Gordy eventually relocated to Detroit in the hope of putting his get rich quick schemes and dreams into reality. A colourful, determined, ambitious personality, he was, despite his chequered past, out to make the big time any which way he could. Berry and school never quite saw eye to eye, and as a result of this he quit high school during the eleventh grade. Shortly after he followed his dream of becoming a professional boxer, which he saw as a well paid route to fame and fortune. However, that was a career that came to a crashing unexpected end when Berry was called up for military service in the army, after which he was shipped overseas to fight in the Korean War in 1952.

From all accounts he was a popular, well-liked soldier, who served in the third infantry divisions artillery. During this time fate stepped in again and he ended up as a chaplain's assistant, driving from service to service and jumping at the chance to play the organ while the chaplain blessed the men about to go into action for a safe return home. One year later, with his tour of duty in Korea under his belt, Berry was shipped back to the States in April 1953, searching out any and every opportunity he could to enable him to start earning money again.

In the same year, and somewhat out of the blue, he married Thelma Coleman, who became the first of his three wives. Shortly after their wedding his passion and love of music, instilled in him by his family from childhood, inspired him to take his first step in the music industry by opening a record store called the 3D Record Mart. Sadly the venture was short lived, forcing Berry to seek out a new opportunity. He ended up working on the automobile production line in the Lincoln Mercury car plant, but the work fell well short of Berry's ambitions. He was already consumed with his burning desire to make it in the music industry any way he could.

After parting company with Lincoln Mercury, through his family connections he was introduced to a man called Al Green (not the same Al Green who went on to become one of the greatest soul artists of all time) who was the owner of a talent club in Detroit called the Flame Show Bar. Now Berry found his first real solid opportunity to break into the music industry. He was introduced to a young Jackie Wilson, who went on to become a legendary soul artist. Unbeknown at the time to Wilson, one of his early hits was a song called 'Reet Petite', a song that was originally penned by Berry and his sister Gwen. It was a song that proved to be much more successful in the UK than the US market.

Despite the single's mixed response, for Berry and Jackie this was the start of a musical writing relationship as the single made it into the stateside R and B charts, as well as the more commercial pop charts, reaching a very respectable number seven. Berry´s successful partnership with Jackie Wilson convinced him that he had what it took to become successful in the music industry. To make this happen he played it cool, sinking the money he earned from his early song writing into discovering and producing talented artists looking for their big break - and there were plenty to choose from in Detroit, where every young black American dreamed of securing a record contract that would set them free from a life of sweat, drudge and noise on the automobile production line.

In 1957, fate smiled on Berry Gordy yet again when he discovered a talented rhythm and blues vocal group called The Miracles, whose co-founder was none other than a young Smokey Robinson, alongside Warren Pete Moore and Ronnie White. The Miracles' career could have all but ended before it began after they ended a disastrous audition with Brunswick Records. Undaunted by this failure, Berry Gordy saw beyond the setback, truly believing that they had the talent to make it to the top; and his belief in them turned out to be well founded.

Fronted by the distinctive, heavenly, soulful voice of Smokey Robinson, who went on to pursue a fantastic successful solo career, The Miracles' repertoire included solid gold songs like 'Shop Around', 'Going To A Go-Go', 'The Tracks Of My Tears', 'I Second That Emotion', 'The Tears Of A Clown' and 'Love Machine'. Berry's belief in them from the beginning was well rewarded as The Miracles provided Tamla Motown with its first million selling single, 'Shop Around'. The group is largely regarded by all those in the know as Motown's first soul super group, with a personal discography boasting twenty-six top forty hits, of which sixteen reached the prestigious *Billboard* top twenty, along with seven top ten singles. 'Tears Of A Clown' claimed the number one spot.

In later life The Miracles were awarded a host of prestigious music industry awards, confirming their awesome talent, including the Pioneer Award from The Rhythm and Blues Foundation, an induction into the Vocal Group Hall of Fame, number thirty-two of *Rolling Stone*'s list of the top one hundred most influential artists, four of their songs entering the Grammy Hall of Fame and a *Billboard* award giving them the sixty-first place on their top one hundred list of the most successful artists ever. And their final accolade in recognition of their truly unique contribution to the music industry was their induction into the Rock and Roll Hall of Fame in 2012.

Following the Miracles' incredible early success, Berry sensed that now was the time to spread his wings and head to the stars. Armed with a family loan of only eight hundred dollars, along with Smokey Robinson's undying belief in his business acumen, Berry created his first record company, calling it Tamla Records and opening for business on the 12th January 1959. Thus the fledgling Tamla Motown was born, with nobody apart from the exception of Berry Gordy himself aware of just how successful Tamla Motown was to become.

"Each day I watched how a bare metal frame rolling down the line would come out the other end a spanking brand new car. What a great deal. Maybe I could do the same with music. Create a place where a kid off the street could walk in one door an unknown, go through a process and come out another door a star." These were Berry Gordy's own words and thoughts while working the Mercury car production line, toying with the idea of building up a musical empire from scratch using the tried and tested methods the automotive bosses applied to making cars - and the rest is history. Although hating the sweat and grime of working the production line, he was hugely impressed with the whole process, and the speed at which the cars rolled off the production line and on to the showroom floor. Did Berry Gordy use factory production techniques in building up his empire? For example he needed a chassis and a body – Hitsville; an engine – the Funk Brothers; a gearbox – the song writers; and a plush interior provided by the artists. Put all those together and Berry Gordy's creation was ready to roll.

The old saying "from little acorns mighty oaks do grow" could have been written with Berry Gordy in mind as he came up with the perfect name for his record company – Motown – Motor City – in recognition of the once great and powerful city Detroit, reflecting the love of the place and the people he'd come to know over the years. Eight hundred dollars was by no stretch of the imagination the kind of capital on which to build the kind of dreams Gordy had, so his approach was both realistic and cautious. He bought a modest building on 2648 West Boulevard comprising of two apartments which eventually became known to the world as Hitsville USA, wedged in between a funeral parlour and a beauty salon, so there was no chance of the neighbours complaining about the music blasting out at all hours. To think that he did everything without a computer, mobile phone, Internet or social networking like Twitter and Instagram makes his achievement even more incredible, with businesses these days taking for granted all those things. The kitchen became the nerve centre of operations, the garage turned into a studio, the lounge took care of banking and bookkeeping and all sales went through the dining room, and it was as simple as that.

He lived with his family in the upstairs apartment, while downstairs he began converting the property into a recording studio known as Studio A, the studio in which so many future Tamla stars cut their recording teeth. Equating Gordy's ideas into automotive terms, Tamla Motown's basic bodywork was complete, so now he was faced with fitting out his dream with a mighty supercharged engine, gearbox and a luxury interior. In order for him to do that, Gordy recruited the assistance of some exceptional people, who were responsible for creating that instantly recognisable Motown sound.

In many places across America in 1959 - Detroit included, despite its sizeable African American population - the country was very much the land of the white man, and nobody was more in tune with that sad reality than Gordy.

Ten years before Gordy created Motown, the music industry labelled music produced or played by black artists as "race music", and it was managed by white recording companies. Gordy smashed through this apartheid-style stronghold by becoming the first black owner of an American music label. His rise to fortune and fame lay in his unusual approach to destroying the colour bar in the music industry. Black audiences might not have supported his approach to solving the problem, because right from the beginning, he never confined himself to strictly black radio stations. His aim was for Motown to appeal to blacks and whites by creating a new kind of pop music, so he could eventually break down the walls of heartache.

In order for him to do that successfully, he knew the secret lay in him employing a top class all-white sales team, men like Al Abrams, who could go into meetings with white executives to sell music performed by black artists. It was all about marketing and winning over the tried and tested stiff competition in order to get Motown into the mainstream, but once that was done, it was only the tip of the iceberg he set about melting. This was a time of simmering racial tensions that affected the country on all levels, and it was tough to come to terms with the reality that the music industry employed all white and all black music venues. When faced with the problem Berry's solution was to purchase a particular venue to allow his artists to perform live.

Because of the permanent white grip on the music industry, Gordy adopted a policy for the eventual greater good of Motown and all his artists. For some it was an unsavoury policy to swallow because it almost reverted back to the days of "yessir no sir" slavery: he instructed his Motown artists on how to look, act and talk whenever they came under the white racist microscope. He made it clear to them that they should stay away from black power and instead become black entertainers, and as unpalatable as his policy was, it worked. Gradually the obnoxious term "black music" became a thing of the past, replaced by the all new fresh sound of rhythm and blues and, of course, soul. Love him or hate him (and plenty did both) for his decision to reduce his artists to the white way of doing business, Berry Gordy and his team pulled off the impossible.

The thought of a black guy starting up a recording label could cause a backlash of jealousy and envy from white folks for even thinking the idea. Gordy needed an ace up his sleeve to take Motown to not only a high level but to make it appealing to all people, cops, criminals, Jews, gypsies, black and white people. Gordy needed a miracle and that was provided in the form of Al Abrams, a fierce white anti-racist who began working for Motown at the tender age of sixteen and eventually became public relations guru for the company. Abrams was Detroit born and bred and entered the world of business instead of college at an early age, which was a decision that would pay huge future dividends for him and a major factor leading him to Hitsville USA due to his love of R and B music, where he faced his first challenge from Gordy. The deal was that if Al was able to manage to get a record on the Zelman label air time on the radio station NCHB, Gordy would give him a job. To Gordy's big surprise, sure enough a short time later Gordy listened to Al's chosen record playing on the radio and gave him a job at a time in the label's development when it could so easily have disappeared without trace.

In a year when the growing Civil Rights Movement was on the march, demanding more equality for African Americans, Al's unceasing work finally broke down so many previously bolted racial doors and he pulled off a gargantuan achievement by getting a black and white photograph of the Supremes on the cover of a television magazine. This was something that had never been done before, for which he was immensely proud. Recalling the ground breaking moment he said: "We saw every magazine cover and article as not just a breakthrough for the Supremes or the Temptations but a breakthrough for the civil rights struggle." It was an incredible achievement, backed up by Martha Reeves admitting that "Al played a big part in helping us to get our music on the radio. Al broke down racial doors. It was his efforts that got us through the doors that were always shut to us."

By 1967 Tamla Motown was well and truly established, leaving Al to part company on good terms to concentrate on creating his own public relations company, doing what he always did best. He boasted a clientele which included James Brown, Holland Dozier Holland and Stax Records in between finding time to work as a journalist and helping to write the musical *Memories Of Motown* featuring the achievements of Berry Gordy based on his best seller autobiography *To Be Loved – The Magic – The Memories Of Motown*. It was a production that to his credit delved into his long term relationships with Diana Ross, Smokey Robinson, Marvin Gaye and Micheal Jackson. The show was overwhelming, recalling so many of Gordy's achievements in the music industry, and finished up on Broadway after enjoying an incredible thirty-seven previews as well as a staggering seven hundred and thirty-eight performances. It earned four nominations at the Tony Awards.

On Sunday October 4th 2015 a tragic loss to the music industry occurred when the legendary Al Abrams died at the age of seventy-two in his home in Ohio after a long, painful battle with cancer. He was Tamla Motown's first ever employee and the man who through his unceasing hard work coined the label's slogan "The Sound of Young America" - and didn't he get that absolutely spot on? RIP Al and God bless you.

Even though Berry Gordy was undoubtably a sharp, ambitious businessman, it is my strong opinion that he would never have made Tamla Motown the kind of success it eventually became without employing Al Abrams. He was, to me, the final piece of the jigsaw, bridging the gap between the constant volatile prejudices prevalent at the time and proving that blacks and whites could work together in harmony to create something so beautiful and lasting. Even after he was diagnosed with cancer, Al was a man who wouldn't stop, telling his wife Nancy to continue his work beyond the grave. He leaves behind him a truly staggering collection of Motown related history together with a collection of photographs and two soon-to-be-published books that are bound to reveal priceless information on what really took place behind the doors of Hitsville USA.

HITSVILLE USA

When it comes to the phrase "unsung heroes" within the music industry, no other musicians can be called that as accurately as the Funk Brothers. Widely regarded as the best by those in the know, the Funk Brothers were Tamla Motown's talented in-house group of musicians from 1959 up until Berry Gordy closed the Detroit operation and relocated to Los Angeles in 1972. In the thirteen years they were together they played on just about every Motown recording you could care to mention, boasting more number one hits than Elvis, the Beach Boys and the Rolling Stones combined. 'My Guy' – 'Where Did Our Love Go' – 'Baby Love' – 'Come See About Me' – 'My Girl' – 'Stop Her On Sight' – 'Stop In The Name Of Love' – 'I Hear A Symphony' – 'Reach Out I'll Be There' – 'You Keep Me Hanging On' – 'Ain't No Mountain High Enough' – 'Just A Little Misunderstanding' – 'Tears Of A Clown' – 'Papa Was A Rolling Stone' – 'Let's Get It On' – 'Shop Around' – 'Reflections' – 'Heat Wave' – 'Standing In The Shadows Of Love' – 'Going To A Go Go' – 'Dancing In The Street' – 'Heaven Must Have Sent You' – 'Cloud Nine' – 'My Cherie Amor' – 'I Second That Emotion' – 'Uptight' – 'Jimmy Mack' – 'It Takes Two' – '25 Miles' – 'War' – 'Don't Walk

Away Renee' – 'Ain't That Peculiar' – the list just goes on and on and certainly warrants the recognition they have now for being one of the reasons why Tamla Motown became so successful.

Earl Van Dyke was born in Detroit in 1930 and became the Funk Brothers' main keyboard player from 1959 to 1972, as well as playing a range of instruments as and when needed. He especially favoured the sound of Fender Rhodes and Hammond with a grand Steinway thrown in for good measure. In 1963, after he completed a successful tour with Aretha Franklin and Lloyd Price Berry, Gordy offered him a contract making him the founder member of the Funk Brothers. In its time the group featured over eighty musicians but boasted a mainstay of thirteen regular members. These were Johnny Griffith on keyboards, Robert White on guitar, Eddie Willis on guitar, Joe Messina on guitar, James Jamerson on bass, Bob Babbitt on bass, Willy Benny Benjamin on drums, Richard Pistol Allen on drums, Uriel Jones on drums, Jack Ashford on percussion, Eddie Bongo Brown on percussion, Jack Ashford on vibraphone and Dave Hamilton on vibraphone and guitar.

Away from the sweaty confines of Studio A Earl Van Dyke was a respected musician, playing with various other artists, including recording for the highly respected jazz label Blue Note alongside saxophonists Ike Quebec and Fred Jackson, as well as releasing numerous of his own recordings. The Funk Brothers spent most of their musical lives in the cramped confines of Studio A, affectionately nicknamed "The Snake Pit", remaining largely anonymous despite the success of Motown until they were all named on Marvin Gaye's hugely successful album *What's Going On.* As we all know, nothing lasts forever, even for the Funk Brothers, who broke up shortly after Gordy closed Hitsville, consigning their invaluable contribution to black American music forever to history. Their longstanding anonymity was exposed to the public even more in the 2002 film *Standing In The Shadows Of Love*, which coincidentally was just what they'd done for many years in Motown.

Following the death of two of the original line up, James Jamerson and Benny Benjamin, the Funk Brothers were finally inducted into the Rock and Roll Hall of Fame in 2000 and 2003 and more awards followed at the forty-fifth Grammy ceremony, when each of their names was read out as the film *Standing In The Shadows Of Motown* took two prizes and the group were given a Lifetime Achievement Award. 2013 saw them leaving their mark on the Hollywood Walk Of Fame, attended by Stevie Wonder and Motown A and R man Mickey Stevenson, whose simple words summed up the music and the professionalism of the Funk Brothers: "The gifts came from upstairs but the touch they formed together." Earl Van Dyke continued enjoying a successful music career away from Studio A and his classic piano based single 'Six by Six' still remains popular to this day. He was a great musician, who died in 1992 aged sixty-two.

Enter the Andantes, a female singing group comprising Jackie Hicks, Marlene Barrow and Luvain Demps, a little known, virtually anonymous Motown group who are reputed to be responsible for providing backing vocals on some twenty thousand recordings, working with Motown's biggest stars. Like the Funk Brothers, they spent most of their musical Motown lives in the bowels of Studio A. They were arguably the most productive artists in the Motown hierarchy, working all year round, and their voices were so good that in the studio they often replaced the original artists whose names appeared on the label before release.

It was common knowledge that the girls were purposely kept in the background by Gordy, who maximised the use of their perfect backing vocals to the full, enabling him to concentrate all his resources on promoting his more successful artists. Gordy's many promises to the girls, promises that he would give them the opportunity to record their own single, for a long time amounted to nothing more than hot air, but finally he relented, and he gave them their chance. The single is called 'Like A Nightmare' and is a fantastic bouncing track full of the Motown magic, written by the immortal song writing trio Holland Dozier Holland and sung by the Andantes on their best form. It should have been the springboard to their fame and fortune, but for many the road to stardom is indeed a rocky and disappointing one. For whatever reason, Motown failed to give it the vital marketing strength needed to make it successful. In the end only a small number of records were pressed and released and sold in and around Detroit's record buying community, bringing to an end the Andantes' solo attempt at the kind of fame and fortune they so richly deserved.

However, for their immense contribution in making Tamla Motown so successful the Andantes were inducted into the Rhythm and Blues Hall of Fame in Carton Ohio in 2014, paying eternal respect to a girl trio who along with the Funk Brothers put the soul into Tamla Motown.

You don't get where Gordy got without making enemies along the way, learning to take the knocks and the rumours and lies that come from jealous minded people. Motown understandably came first with Gordy, and he expected his musicians and artists to be full of the same passion. The music industry was a fragile beast back then, fraught with constant financial problems. His musicians wanted paying for their work, and it was hard trying to balance the books to keep Motown afloat as well finding a chunk of cash to sink into what he thought was going to be the next big thing. Royalties were frequently paid late and recording work was nowhere near as well paid as going on tours and playing live, which is what a number of artists did to keep them afloat. Gordy strongly disapproved of this and when he found out that the Funk Brothers, who were an irreplaceable part in the Motown machine, were doing it he was so annoyed that he fined them a thousand dollars. It was clear proof that he was not going to allow anyone, no matter who they were, to rock the Motown boat.

In later years there were the frequent well documented heated arguments between him and Marvin Gaye, who eventually quit Motown for deeply personal reasons. Gordy had always made it clear to his Motown hierarchy that they should stay away from Civil Rights issues, but Marvin Gaye's worldwide successful 1971 album *What's Going On* openly challenged what was happening in America, especially the Vietnam War, in which his brother was fighting. He just couldn't put up with Gordy's rigid, outdated attitude any longer. The title track of the album was written by Four Tops bass player Renaldo Obie Benson, who was in San Francisco when he witnessed brutal police violence towards a group of hippies.

What was Gordy thinking, letting an artist like Marvin Gaye leave the fold, knowing he was never going to find another artist comparable to him? For me it was one of the biggest mistakes he ever made, contributing to the eventual end of Motown. Edwin Starr's 1970 album *War and Peace* was clearly a protest against the Vietnam War, urging people of all race and colour to come together as one. 'War' was one of the first Motown songs to address the serious state of the troubled politics of the day. It was first offered to the Temptations until Gordy changed his mind, fearing that it would turn Motown into a controversial peace movement record label; he gave it to Edwin Starr as his fan base wasn't as big, which meant it wouldn't hurt him financially as much.

Gordy had many great ideas which he used to make Tamla Motown successful, especially during the all-important precarious early days when it could have crashed and burned. Unlike the majority of recording companies who went to the expense of paying professional session men to record for them, Gordy went to extreme measures to make sure he kept everything in house as much as he could, in order to save cash he could use elsewhere. This meant that all those in the Motown hierarchy had to be fully prepared to roll up their shirt and blouse sleeves and get down to perfecting the art of multi and often triple tasking, with the exception of the Funk Brothers and the Andantes who were virtually permanent residents within the confines of Studio A.

No two days were the same, meaning that Marvin could be writing a song for Brenda Holloway, Smokey singing on a Frank Wilson track, the Four Tops providing additional backing vocals alongside the Andantes, who could find themselves slipping into the Supremes' shoes, with even Gordy frequently adding his writing and production skills. Such was the professionalism, friendship, awareness and sense of destiny they all shared in Hitsville at that time, from the boss down; and what magical, creative days and nights they must have been. It was musical socialism at the highest possible peak, which no doubt helped to cement Tamla Motown's success.

Enter Norman Whitfield, who many people testify was a leading influence in making Motown successful, eventually pushing it into a new direction which Gordy often disagreed with. A simple twist of fate saw him arrive in Detroit after his father's car broke down. He was only eighteen and already a prolific writer and producer for Detroit's Thelma Records when he became a massive fan of Berry Gordy and what he was trying to achieve. With increasing spare time on his hands in an all new environment offering all kinds of possibilities, Norman began hanging around the Motown office hoping that Gordy would give him his dream job, so Gordy hired him in 1962. After familiarising himself with the way his new boss took care of business, he was appointed to run the quality control department, with the big responsibility of listening to and selecting those songs he thought were good enough for Motown while binning the rest, in between working alongside Harvey Fuqua and Holland Dozier Holland collaborating on the single 'I Couldn't Cry If I Wanted To' for the Temptations, who he shared a close working relationship with during his time at Motown.

His huge natural talent for spotting potential hits was quickly recognised by Gordy, who chose him to work alongside the company's hardworking songwriting team, working alongside Marvin Gaye, the Marvelettes, and the Temptations from 1966 up until 1974. He was recognised as the man who singlehandedly changed the sound of the Temptations from their tried and tested classic soul sound to a much more altogether different darker psychedelic sound, as was clearly demonstrated with one of their biggest successes 'Cloud Nine', a record that earned Motown their first ever Grammy Award for Best Rhythm and Blues Performance by a Group. Five years later they were awarded a second Grammy for their global hit 'Pappa Was A Rolling Stone'. The biggest single success of his career was 'War', released by Edwin Starr, and two more albums for the Temptations, *All Directions* and *Masterpiece*, which came at a crucial time when Motown was on the decline due to a number of expensive film projects with little to show for the investment.

Norman Whitfield's individual influence changed much of the traditional sound of Motown forever, placing much more emphasis on the music as opposed to letting the vocals do the work, and it was a change that created a lot of friction and arguments with a number of artists who didn't want to go down the new route, the Temptations included, despite their new found success and recognition. Inevitably Whitfield and Motown parted company, thereby giving him the freedom and direction to start his own company operating under his own name and working with a number of former Motown stars. More success followed with his big hit 'Car Wash' recorded by Edwin Starr's former backing band Rose Royce earning him yet another Grammy award for Best Original Score, after which a brief return to Motown in the 1980s saw him produce the album *Sail Away* for the Temptations.

His later years were troubled ones, falling foul of the Inland Revenue Service, which fined him over twenty thousand dollars for non-payment of tax. Suffering from various ailments, including acute diabetes, the man who played such a vital role in the early development of Tamla Motown died on September 16th 2008, age sixty-five, of diabetes.

Barrett Strong was a naturally talented performer and songwriter who was born in Mississippi in 1941. From an early age it was clear he was gravitating towards becoming a professional musician, singing and playing piano. A case of not what you know but who you know occurred when he was spotted playing in Detroit by none other than Jackie Wilson, who was so impressed with the young man that he organised a meeting with Gordy. His second single, 'Money', was a big success, taking the number two spot on the R and B chart as well as featuring in the top thirty of the pop chart. 'Money' proved to be such a powerful song that it was later covered by the Beatles, the Stones, the Doors, Little Richard and Pearl Jam.

His follow up single failed to emulate the success of 'Money' so he quit Motown and headed for Philadelphia, writing and recording for respected labels like Atco, Cameo Parkway, Veejay and Okeh. A return to Detroit saw him back working with Norman Whitfield, recording a new version of the classic Motown hit 'I Heard It Through The Grapevine'. The song was first recorded by Gladys Knight before Marvin Gaye took it to number one. It was the track that eventually provided the background music to the steamy Levi jeans launderette advert responsible for sending young girls' blood pressures sky high as the young toned and tanned hunk Nick Kamen suggestively slithered out of his jeans and put them in the washing machine, leaving him wearing only a pair of white boxer shorts. Barrett Strong is still involved in the music industry as a songwriter and performer.

There can be no discussion of Motown without mentioning the legendary songwriting trio Holland Dozier Holland. Eddie Holland was the brother of Brian Holland, who alongside Lamont Dozier wrote so many of Motown's earliest and many say greatest hits. Originally a talented performer in his own right with a number of hits to his name, Eddie suffered badly from stage fright, forcing him to give up his love of singing. He preferred to work behind the scenes, concentrating on writing songs. Once Gordy had the bodywork in place, the next to be fitted was the engine supplied by the legendary Motown trio of Holland Dozier Holland, Brian and Lamont responsible for composing and producing, leaving Eddie to concentrate on taking care of the lyrics and vocal arrangements.

Between 1962 and 1967, the legendary trio produced so many songs that many people, myself included, regard these as the absolute classic years of Detroit Tamla Motown. They were responsible for twenty-five number one songs, composed over four hundred songs, had one hundred and thirty pop charts hits, and seventy top ten hits, forty of which reached number one. Regrettably I feel that their five years at Motown were nowhere near enough; they left to set up their own record labels, Invictus and Hot Wax, because they claimed Gordy had failed to pay them long overdue royalties. Not only that; they also claimed that he'd actually forged their signatures on a number of contracts, preventing them from using their material in their own names, signalling the beginning of a very long and painful legal battle which lasted some thirty years. They summed it up in the following words: "Business is business, love is love."

The success of their songs was endless, providing fame and fortune for so many future stars who walked through the doors of Hitsville USA hoping to secure a deal that would provide the escape from the sweat and exhaustion of the endless auto production line and change their lives forever. They wrote hits for so many: Mary Wells – the Marvelettes – Martha and her Vandellas – the Miracles before and after Smokey Robinson – the Supremes – the Temptations – Jimmy Ruffin - the Four Tops – R Dean Taylor – Brenda Holloway – Barbara McNair – Junior Walker and his All Stars – the Isley Brothers – Kim Weston – Edwin Starr – Dionne Warwick – Stevie Wonder.

All these and many more artists enjoyed the high life thanks to the immense talents of Holland Dozier Holland. Between 1963 and 1990, over thirty of their songs made it to the *Billboard* Top Ten, making them one of the most acclaimed song writing and producing teams in musical history. More recognition of their talents followed, including them being inducted into the Songwriters Hall of Fame in 1988, followed five years later with their induction into the Rock and Roll Hall of Fame. In 2009 they were awarded the Johnny Mercer Award from the Songwriters Hall of Fame and in 2015 they were awarded a star on the Hollywood Walk of Fame. They were also awarded the National Academy of Songwriters Lifetime Achievement Award with their names being inscribed next to some auspicious company including Lennon and McCartney, Duke Ellington, George Gershwin and others.

Add the name of the one and only Smokey Robinson to the Motown songwriting team and how could Gordy fail to become successful? With a career in music stretching back over five decades, Smokey is credited with writing over a staggering four thousand songs, an achievement earning him praise from another great artist, Bob Dylan, who once called him "America's greatest poet". Detroit born and bred, Smokey was still in high school when he came up with the idea of creating the Miracles, the group that went on to become Gordy's very first vocal group, and as legend has it, it was actually Smokey's idea that Gordy create the name Tamla Motown. The Miracles' first ever single, 'Shop Around', hit number one on the R and B charts and it was this that started the avalanche of future hits, led by Smokey's effortless, distinctive silk-smooth vocal style.

'Ooo Baby, You've Really Got A Hold Of Me', 'The Tracks Of My Tears', 'Going To A Go Go', 'More Love', 'Tears Of A Clown', 'I Second That Emotion' - all these early massively successful singles, penned by Smokey Robinson, helped to keep the Miracles as the number one group on the R and B music scene, earning Gordy millions. At the same time Smokey was fiercely loyal to the man who'd given him his big break, who in turn repaid his friendship and loyalty by appointing him Vice President of Tamla Motown records after he left the Miracles. He became the label's talent scout, songwriter and producer, giving him the chance to really come into his own, writing and producing songs for the Temptations, Brenda Holloway, Mary Wells, Marvin Gaye and many more artists. Everyone hoped for the chance to record one of Smokey Robinson's in-demand songs.

Smokey Robinson cared for Tamla Motown just as much as Gordy did, and he continued to remain at Gordy's side, guiding and advising him on what and what not to do, right up until he sold the company. That was a move that ended what I consider to be a truly unique partnership in the history of the African American music industry. Leaving Motown pushed Smokey into a new solo career and he released a number of albums, laced with his instantly recognisable voice, as well as performing to audiences worldwide. As to his awards and achievements, it would be a far easier task to list what he hasn't won, both with the Miracles and as a solo songwriter/producer/performer.

Rolling Stone listed the Miracles at number thirty-two on their one hundred greatest artists of all time – *Billboard* listed them as seventy-one on theirs – they were four times inducted into the Grammy Hall of Fame, winning more Grammy Hall of Fame inductions than any other Motown group – *Rolling Stone* listed 'Ooo Baby', 'Tracks Of My Tears' and 'Shop Around' in their five hundred greatest songs of all time list and *Going To A Go Go* in their five hundred greatest albums of all time list, plus a place in their one hundred greatest artists of all time list – Rock and Roll Hall of Fame's list of five hundred songs that shaped rock and roll included 'Going To A Go Go', 'Tracks Of My Tears', 'Shop Around' and 'You've Really Got A Hold Of Me' – they were inducted into the Vocal Group Hall of Fame – given a place on the Hollywood Walk of Fame – inducted into the Grammy Hall of Fame – inducted into the Doo Wop Hall of Fame – inducted into the Michigan Rock and Roll Legends Hall of Fame. It's all a truly magnificent achievement for the young kid who grew up in the Brewster Douglas housing project on the outskirts of Detroit, the kind of desperate place where residents dream about escaping, but few make it out. Smokey, who earned the nickname Smokey Joe from his uncle Claude after his obsession for watching cowboy westerns, escaped into enormous fame and success.

On October 14th 2013, aged 98, Maxine Powell died. She was the woman about whom Diana Ross publicly admitted "she taught me everything I know." Maxine Powell moved to Detroit in 1945, teaching classes in modelling and self-improvement. Some six years later she managed to purchase a large house in the city and called it The Maxine Powell Finishing and Modelling School. Her speciality was searching out talented African Americans to come and work in theatre companies both in Detroit and across America, as well as grabbing any opportunity that came along to get her clients recognised by securing them paid advertising campaigns.

Her glitzy, glamorous style and frequent fashion shows soon became the talk of the Detroit social calendar, attracting celebrities from across the city, which is where she met Berry Gordy, a man with a few burning ambitions of his own to achieve. The two of them struck up an instant friendship and in 1964 Maxine closed her school after Gordy offered her a consultancy at the Motown office. She became solely responsible for the day to day running of the company's artist personal development department.

Always with his eye firmly focused on the future success of his beloved Motown, Gordy's musical policy was a simple one. It had to appeal to everyone, black or white. Once the music sounded good, he insisted that his artists looked even better, because they were firmly in the public and media eye, representing Motown wherever they were seen. Those fabulous nostalgic black and white stills and posters depicting attractive, smiling, elegant, immaculately dressed young men and women were not just simply thrown together. They were in fact part of a perfectly orchestrated advertisement campaign featuring the fresh new face of African American soul music, and central to that plan was Maxine Powell, whose job it was to groom the new stars to perfection.

The woman who reputedly taught Marvin Gaye to sing with his eyes open had one central, effective, simple philosophy. Bearing in mind that many of the budding Motown stars came from rough backgrounds, armed with attitudes and language they'd learned from birth in order to survive life on the street, Maxine was left with more than her fair share of work to do to iron out their many creases until they met both her and Gordy's exacting standards. She expressed this in the following words: "Some were rude and crude but my purpose was to help the Motown artists to become classy both on and off the stage because it's not where you come from, it's where you're going that counts. Some were rude and crude but when you're black and on show you cannot afford to fail. All my life I was thinking of things that would help my race to become outstanding and I thought of class and style. Two things that would be accepted around the world and I know that to look chic, stunning, elegant and smart can be learnt." And I for one, Miss Powell, wholeheartedly agree with your philosophy in life that you can overcome anything providing you have that determination and self-belief.

Maxine Powell taught many of her artists the art of personal grooming coupled with social graces, with Berry Gordy insisting that even his most successful touring artists still had to attend the artist development programme whenever they returned to Hitsville USA; and over the course of time it worked. Martha Reeves and Smokey Robinson both agreed that "Maxine was a lady of immense grace, elegance and style and we did our best to emulate her. I don't think we would have been as successful at all without her training and it worked."

Maxine died in the presence of some of her beloved Motown family, living by the code she practised all her life. A lady whose strict advice was vitally important for her people summed it up in the following words: "I teach class and class will turn the heads of kings and queens."

Inevitably with that number of artists signed to Tamla Motown, some displaying certain lifestyles, temperaments and attitudes more than others, one or two were eventually going to fall by the wayside, and Barbara McNair was one such example. She was one of my all-time favourite singers to come out of Hitsville USA and an artist that presented the same kind of ongoing problems to Berry Gordy as the late great much troubled footballing genius George Best did to his all-forgiving manager and mentor the late great Sir Matt Busby. Born in Chicago in 1934, it was clear from an early age that Barbara was going to blossom into a successful artist who looked and sang the part more than most young girls dreaming of fortune and fame.

After finishing her education, Barbara auditioned for a place at the prestigious American Music Conservatory, hungry for the kind of success all budding artists dream about. Her big break into showbiz came early when she was offered a spot on the popular *Arthur Godfrey's Talent Scouts* television show, earning her regular spots in clubs like the Purple Onion, the Coconut Grove and the Persian Room where she became instantly recognised as "a gorgeous young woman with a warm easy communicative personality and a voice that can range from softly intense ballads to the edges of gospel" as one journalist from New York wrote about her.

Barbara released her first single 'Till There Was You' with Coral Records back in 1958, which led to her joining the mighty Nat King Cole on a world tour, in addition to which she accepted his invitation to appear with him in two Broadway shows he wrote called *The Merry World of Nat King Cole* and *I'm With You*. Barbara soon became a popular, well-loved artist endearing herself to the nation's hearts even more by agreeing to join Bob Hope on a morale boosting tour of Vietnam, entertaining the troops, before driving every red blooded American male crazy when she posed nude on the cover of *Playboy* magazine. A string of television successes soon followed when she was given a part in the popular noir crime drama *If He Hollers Then Let Him Go* as well as appearing in *Doctor Kildare* and three of my television favourites back in the day, *I Spy*, *Hogan's Heroes* and *Mission Impossible*. More success followed when she gave a memorable appearance playing Sydney Poitier's wife in the racially charged Hollywood classic *They Call Me Mister Tibbs* and even got the chance to swivel her hips alongside The King in his last film *Change of Habit*. In 1969 her recognition as an accomplished versatile artist earned her the previously unthinkable honour of becoming the first black female artist to host her own television show, appropriately titled *The Barbara McNair Show* and featuring the likes of Freda Payne, Johnny Mathis, Lou Rawls, BB King, Debbie Reynolds, Little Richard, Sonny and Cher and one of the finest, most instantly recognisable silky smooth voices around, that of the one and only Tony Bennett.

Her natural, sexy, sophisticated style soon brought her to the attention of Berry Gordy, who saw in Barbara the talent to equal if not better the likes of the mighty Diana Ross and Martha Reeves, recording many of the songs Diana Ross turned down. Her one big single, for which she will always be remembered, is 'You're Gonna Love My Baby'. It was a single that said it all about her unique sound and a single that became a monster northern soul anthem and an automatic dance floor filler to this day.

Sadly, with genius there is often a price to pay, and Barbara's personal life was so troubled that it affected the one true thing she was born to do. Her marriages included the Funk Brothers' main musician Earl Wright, which lasted some seven years before she moved on to Jack Rafferty, Frederick Andrews and Andrew "Manzie", which turned out to be a disastrous marriage just waiting to happen. Manzie was a Mafia associate, claiming that he had some big connections to the mob. By this time Barbara was enjoying a flirtation with heroin, which hit public headlines in 1972 when both she and her husband were charged with possession. Four years later, during an appearance in a Chicago nightclub, Barbara was given the shock news that her husband had been killed, shot six times in a gangland style killing in their home. A former Mafia boss turned police informer eventually testified that Manzie was killed because he attempted to put out a contract on an established tax law attorney who was seen as detrimental to Mafia affairs. Before his death Barbara had hit the headlines again, found in possession of heroin at the Playboy club in New Jersey. She had signed for a package containing the drug, but she claimed in court that she had no knowledge of the contents of the parcel and all charges were dropped against her. Her husband Manzie was later charged with the offence.

In 1987 Barbara filed for bankruptcy for close to five hundred thousand dollars, the equivalent of a cool million in modern day currency, and her later years saw her living in Los Angeles, content with her surroundings, playing tennis and going skiing to keep her active in between the few and far between tours. During her tours around America Barbara experienced the very worst racism, suffering obscene phone calls, verbal abuse and hate mail. She was once refused permission to swim in the pool in the hotel where she was staying and was forced to eat with the hotel staff because blacks weren't allowed in the main dining room.

That was truly unspeakable, horrendous treatment of an artist once described as one of the most beautiful women in the world. Barbara McNair died in LA from throat cancer on February 4th 2007, aged seventy-two years old. One of the true soul divas who never quite matched her potential, much loved and missed by all those who were touched by her music.

TAMLAS IN TOWN

All credit where credit is due. No mention of the early rise of the UK Tamla Motown scene can be made without mentioning Mister Dave Godin. A seemingly ordinary, unobtrusive man who was anything but; when it came to the subject of soul music, a man I met ever so briefly and shook hands with in the cauldron of Wigan Casino - he was there to see for himself what the place and the music was all about in readiness for a feature he was writing for *Blues and Soul* magazine, in which he recalled that he "really enjoyed" himself.

Without doubt one of the world's premier authorities on all kinds of soul music, he worked hard to popularise it in the UK. Whether or not the charming original story of how he actually discovered the music happens to be true or not, it certainly makes for amusing reading. Dave the young teenager from Bexley Heath was seconds away from experiencing a life changing moment when he walked into an ice cream parlour; a bunch of builders were taking a rest there, listening to some soul music blasting out from an American jukebox, and one track in particular, by singer Ruth Brown called 'Mamma He Treats Your Daughter Mean', caught his ear.

As the story goes, Dave was so desperate to catch the title, he sat there swivelling his head around in order to read the details on the label; as he recalls in his own words: "I was trying to read the label as it went round and round and a bloke saw that I was interested and pointed it out on the jukebox list. It was earthy, so real and the words so adult. This young man – I wish I could go back and thank him now because it changed my life – gave me five sixpences and said that if you like this, then you'll also like this. It's called rhythm and blues, black American music."

From the tiniest of acorns mighty oaks often grow and so Dave Godin's passion and love of soul music began in earnest. After leaving grammar school he travelled around the States listening and educating himself to as much music as possible, during which time he also became a lifelong vegetarian. On his return to the UK he adamantly refused to agree to National Service and convinced the ruling committee so much as to his reasons why that he was allowed to serve two years working as a hospital porter; but that failed to divert him from his true mission in life.

1963 was the year when Dave created the Tamla Motown Appreciation Society, with some help from Margaret Phelps, who was president of the Hitsville International Fan Club. Upon joining, every member of the society received a pin badge to wear with pride, along with a membership card; over the course of time these have become rare, sought-after collectable items due to the fact there were only about three hundred members. They also received Tamla Motown letters, with all the latest news on what was happening in Hitsville. The young non-stereotypical Dave Godin managed to weave his way into the Motown hierarchy so far that he was given the privilege of entertaining people like Smokey Robinson's wife Claudette and two of the Marvelettes, Catherine Anderson and Gladys Horton.

Despite all his tireless efforts he was surprised to discover that the UK Tamla labels expressed scant interest in his ideas. Undeterred, in his typical Dave Godin way of solving problems, he changed an unacceptable negative into a truly fantastic positive when he eventually received a detailed telegram from none other than the man himself, Berry Gordy, who invited him to an all-expenses-paid visit to Detroit with a view to discussing plans for Tamla Motown's commercial expansion into the UK market. Throughout the visit Gordy listened intently to Dave's ideas, probing him for advice on what and what not to release as the next potential big hit, and by the time the pair shook hands and said goodbye until the next time, Gordy rewarded Dave's wealth of knowledge by giving him a job as a paid consultant for the rapidly expanding Motown empire. Dave returned home patting himself on the back for a job well done.

His love of the music fuelled an even deeper passion for championing the cause in the UK, and to spread the word, he set up his own UK Tamla Motown label. This proved to be a success thanks to his decision to popularise the complete sound of Motown, instead of any one particular artist who risked being the flavour of the month before they disappeared without trace. Now working for Tamla Motown, success lay at Dave's feet, and you would have thought that he would have been pleased with all the publicity building up at the time in readiness for the eagerly awaited Tamla Motown revue about to hit the UK. Nobody could have been behind the idea as much as Dave Godin, but his gut feeling convinced him to take an opposing stance, warning Gordy that now was not the best time to stage such a spectacular show. Gordy, being the man he was, who rarely took no for an answer from anybody, never mind his employees, went ahead with the revue, which turned into a financial disaster, with only the London shows packed out.

Undeterred by his setbacks with Gordy, the soul pilgrim continued on his merry way, opening a record shop in Deptford in 1967 before moving to a second larger one in Monmouth Street, Covent Garden, called appropriately enough Soul City Records, from where he preached the gospel of soul to his increasing flock of devotees. His partners in crime were two young guys, Dave Nathan (the founder member of the Nina Simone Appreciation Society) and Rob Blackmore, who were massively into black American music and came up with the idea of creating the Soul City record label to help supply the increasing demand from their discerning customers searching for a new sound.

The shop was painted in distinctive magenta and blue, which were also the colours they used for their Soul City label, with every single carrying the words "soul as deep as you like and then some"; the very same words the legendary northern soul deejay used to front his popular Sunday soul music radio show back in the day. It was around this time that the shop staff were being inundated by customers – predominantly northern football supporters in London for the weekend who were buying singles as fast as they could get their hands on them. When staff asked Dave what kind of soul music they were selling, he told them to call it northern soul, and thus another legend based around Tamla Motown was born - in a terribly British way.

Initially distributed by Island and Phillips records, Soul City possessed all the knowledge, integrity and connections to become successful; but sadly this was not to be. The love and the passion for the music far outweighed the financial stability which would ensure the label's survival, and so regrettably Soul City records closed in 1976. The label had released some twenty singles, from artists such as Billy Butler, Major Lance, Billy Preston, Chris Jackson, Erma Franklin, Don Gardner and Gene Chandler, who all went on to enjoy successful careers in their own right.

This lifelong dedicated pioneer of black American soul music died in Rotherham, Yorkshire, peacefully in his sleep, aged sixty-eight, on Friday October 15th 2004. RIP Mister Dave Godin, soulman extraordinaire and then some.

And so it was that in the spring of 1965 Berry Gordy, acting against Dave Godin's cautious advice, decided to send some of his biggest stars to perform in the UK at The Tamla Motown Revue. Under an explosion of media interest, Motown's finest arrived in London on the 16th of March, four days before the tour kicked off in earnest, with their first appearance the following Saturday at the Finsbury Park Astoria. This was quickly followed by an additional two shows the next night at the Hammersmith Odeon, before embarking on a mammoth whirlwind nationwide tour playing over twenty theatres twice a night, as well as somehow finding the time to appear on a one-off specially recorded live session for the popular television show *Ready Steady Go*. The show was the brainchild of two Motown fanatics, Vicki Wickham and our own queen of soul Dusty Springfield, who could bang a tune out as well as any of her American sisters and brothers and who had already appeared with Martha Reeves, Marvin Gaye, the Isley Brothers and the one and only Kim Weston, who later on in her career became a much loved queen of the 70s northern soul scene with her anthem 'Helpless' considered by many, me included, to be one of the greatest soul singles ever recorded.

For just four pounds fifteen shillings the increasing army of UK soul fans got see the artists they'd only heard on vinyl perform live. They could see Martha Reeves and the Vandellas, Smokey Robinson and the Miracles, Stevie Wonder, who was only fourteen at the time, and topping the bill the Supremes with the Temptations, who flew into the UK to perform with the backing music provided by the Earl

Van Dyke Six, who were part of Tamla Motown's legendary Funk Brothers. The revue was Gordy's attempt to really break into the UK soul market, but surprisingly things didn't go as planned. With London being the epicentre of the Mod scene, venues outside of the capital were poorly attended, despite the appearance of the hugely popular Georgie Fame and his Blue Flames who had topped the charts at the time with his signature single 'Yeah Yeah'.

On the Rolling Stones tour in 1965 - and they were already an established group - the most expensive tickets came in close to twelve shillings, whereas ticket prices for the Motown Revue were anywhere between ten and seventeen and six, in places across the country where people earned considerably less than people did in London. On the plus side, if you were a diehard Motown fan, determined to follow your idols across the country, the lack of interest in ticket sales guaranteed you could buy a ticket; so it was very much a case of some you win some you lose for Motown, who took on a punishing schedule that few artists today would contemplate.

It was intense: 20th March – Astoria Finsbury Park – 21st March – Hammersmith Odeon – 23rd March – Colston Hall Bristol – 24th March - Capital Cardiff – 25th March – Odeon Birmingham – 26th March – ABC Kingston – 27th March – Winter Gardens Bournemouth – 28th March – Odeon Leicester – 30th March – Odeon Manchester – 31 March – Odeon Leeds – 1 April – Odeon Glasgow – 2 April – Odeon Stockton – 3 April – City Hall Newcastle – 4 April – Empire Liverpool – 6 April – ABC Luton – 7 April – ABC Chester – 8 April – City Hall Sheffield – 9 April – ABC Wigan – 10 April – Gaumont Wolverhampton – 11 April – Gaumont Ipswich – 12 April – Guildhall Portsmouth, the final night of the Motown Revue, during which the artists had only three days off in a total of forty-two appearances.

For Berry Gordy and his Motown stars, the Revue amounted to nothing less than a complete financial disaster; but to his single minded way of thinking, it was the price he willingly paid for introducing his stars to the UK market, a tough nut to crack. His persistence eventually paid off thanks to hits like 'Superstition' by Stevie Wonder, 'Going to a Go-Go' by Smokey Robinson and 'Reach Out I'll Be There' by the Four Tops, who by then were well on their way to worldwide fortune and fame. The Beatles' manager Brian Epstein paid what was reputed to be a fortune for them to headline at his twelve hundred seat venue the Saville Theatre, performing a gig that was claimed to be the best they ever played; and they played a lot during their career.

Tamla Motown was here to stay, with many classic Detroit based tracks still played today at soul nights across the country, recalling countless memories for all of us and sounding as fresh and vibrant as they did when they were first released over fifty years ago. It was a magical time before old age started to take its toll on our once energetic dancefloor moves. On a personal note, I can't imagine pulling up at a petrol station on my Lambretta SX200, cold, shivering and hungry, the moment the Motown tour bus arrived and out stepped the likes of Martha Reeves, the Supremes, Stevie Wonder and the Earl Van Dyke Six taking time out to stretch their tired legs before grabbing a Wimpey burger and fries. What a memory that would have been.

MOTOWN OR MOBTOWN?

In 1916 a black man was lynched in Cedarbluff Mississippi by a mob baying for blood. His only crime was that he accidentally touched the shoulder of a white woman running to catch his train, but the incensed mob saw the incident as nothing less than the rape of a white woman by a black man. In the period from 1882 to 1968 figures amounting to some 4,743 lynchings took place across the US, out of which 3,346 were black people. In 2018 in Alabama, recognition of these atrocities took the shape of the National Memorial for Peace and Justice, which stands close to where the old Montgomery market once stood, where thousands of terrified Africans were brought to be displayed and sold off to the highest bidders. Over eight hundred suspended steel sheets are engraved with the names of all the counties where lynchings occurred along with the names, where possible, of all those murdered.

One of those was a young African American named Mack Charles Parker, aged twenty-three, who was arrested for the alleged rape of a white woman in Poplarville Mississippi on April 24th 1959. He was held in the local courthouse before being transferred to jail, but mob mentality took over and the young man was dragged from his cell before the mob beat and shot him, dumping his body in the Pearl River a few miles out of town. Following a rushed rudimentary FBI investigation into his murder, it wasn't at all surprising that those responsible for his murder were set free, as was the case with many such incidents. For me it's important to highlight the very real and constant danger Black Americans were subjected to: segregated, abused, beaten and murdered. Another time and place and that could have been Mister Motown murdered for no real reason. This racism was rife across America; in Detroit Martha Reeves once recalled being held at gunpoint by a policeman for being audacious enough to use a "whites only" toilet, and it was common knowledge that members of the Temptations, Four Tops and other Motown stars frequently carried arms to protect themselves whenever they were out for the night.

From the many black and white photographs I've studied of Detroit back in the day, it looked a fabulous place to live, easily equalling many other US cities, with a fantastic selection of building styles from art deco, modernism, classical and Italian renaissance, and the gigantic Grand Street station looked like something from Gotham City. Detroit at night was equally fabulous; people dressed in their best weekend clothes and headed down town for a few beers and a meal and then danced the night away in one of the original glamorous ballrooms that were on offer: The Vanity, the Grande, the Greystone, the Fox Theatre and the Dancery along with the Twenty Grand club, where future Motown artists performed, and the Rooster Tail set on the river where Aretha Franklin, Tony Bennett and the Rolling Stones once played - and the place where Berry Gordy spent a lot of his time in between checking out new acts.

Detroit was also a dangerous city, where a person could get killed or seriously injured for venturing into the wrong neighbourhood. As in most US cities the Mafia's presence was strong, having been established since they first started arriving back in the early 1900s. Officially they were known as the Tocco Zerilli family or the Detroit Partnership and their power was ruthless and absolute, being one of the top twenty-four families that belonged to the Cosa Nostra. Originally from Sicily, Giacomo Tocco and Joe Zerilli subjected Detroit to a reign of terror for years, carrying out single and multiple murders and fighting turf wars with any rivals who dared to stand in their way.

Joseph Zerilli was the actual family boss between 1936 and 1972, dealing out murder and extortion and buying up property and partnerships in nightclubs in the city. What really made them so unique is the fact that they preferred to marry within the family ranks, making themselves a highly trusted well-oiled machine willing to go all the way and then some for the love and honour of the family. In 2014 and 2015 the family suffered an enormous setback forcing them to keep a low profile after the deaths of Tocco and Zerilli. In 1975 they were in the spotlight as well as being under the scrutiny of the police after they were accused of the murder of Jimmy Hoffa, which nobody has proved even to this day. Hoffa was the controversial union boss who disappeared never to be seen again. Speculation is still rife today as to what exactly happened to him on the 30th July 1975, the day he disappeared forever. What has been confirmed is that Hoffa had arranged to meet two big time Mafia men in a restaurant downtown, Jack Giacalone and Tony Provenzano, in a bid to repair their differences. A truck driver claims he saw Jimmy Hoffa being driven off in the back seat of a car sitting next to a man who appeared to be holding a long object. More rumours claim that Jimmy Hoffa is buried in the cement foundations of the Giants stadium, making them not the kind of people you want to testify against.

By the time Berry Gordy arrived in Detroit to begin his dream, the Mafia had started moving on recording companies, sensing that music was going to be the next best thing, and offering them a deal they couldn't turn down or buying them out altogether, forcing their artists to come and work for them - and what artist could possibly say no? Stan The Man, the creator of Philly Groove records, went one step better and actually turned to the notorious Black Mafia for help, using intimidation and violence to help expand his business. Three more record labels, Meltone Music, White Music and Jaycee Music were co-owned by the notorious Mafia gangsters Vince Meli, who was only twenty-four when he moved into the music business, Mike Pollizi and Rafael Quasarano, who controlled most of the jukeboxes in Detroit as well as paying nightclub owners visits with the intention of persuading them to promote certain artists signed to their labels, using intimidation and threats of violence. Vince Meli, the Mafia underboss of the crime family in Detroit, didn't start out a gangster. Originally from Sicily his family came to the US in the 1920s and Meli earned a degree from Notre Dame University Indiana before enlisting in the army. He served with distinction in the Second World War, as well as taking part in Operation Overlord, the invasion of France on that fateful June morning back in 1944. He was a tough soldier by all accounts, who returned home to Detroit where he began his life of crime with the mob.

But the Mafia weren't the only seriously dangerous criminals in Detroit back then. Two African Americans who came from poor, humble backgrounds rose to become the biggest heroin dealers in the city. Eddy Fat Man Jackson was born and bred in Detroit and wanted the kind of luxurious life he was never going to get by working in an ordinary job, so he started dealing heroin, eventually becoming the biggest dealer in the city. Courtney Brown was a former busman who wanted the same things as Eddie and eventually became his second in command, given the task of taking care of most of the logistical details the firm had. It was around this time when an incident happened to Berry Gordy that would remain with him forever more - and that was the mystery surrounding the question of whether he accepted a loan from the Mafia when they made him the offer "we want half of Motown or you'll have all of nothing."

He swears to this day that he did not accept that offer - but how could he not? These were ruthless criminals who wanted a piece of Motown, and I cannot believe for one second that he turned down the cash to keep them off his back. One thing I've always admired and respected about Berry Gordy was that he kept control of Motown right up until the time he moved to Los Angeles, where financial problems got the better of him and he was forced to sell Motown. Did he make enough cash from the talents of Smokey, Marvin, Diana, the Four Tops, the Temptations and all the other artists to stay in business or did he take the quick route and sell off a piece of Motown to the Mafia? Many people who were there back in the day believe he took the cash; and there are just as many who swear he didn't. It's something we will never know, a truth that Gordy will take to the grave; but my question to him would be: just how do you turn men down like that, men who don't take no for an answer? How do you turn them down, knowing that if you do, there's a good chance you'll end up in the foundations of the Giants stadium alongside Jimmy Hoffa?

There were a number of Motown artists who had connections to the Mafia that could have possibly helped to get inside Hitsville, all unconfirmed, but there's no smoke without fire. In 1964 the Mafia were actively chasing to buy Mary Wilson after she had left the Supremes and her career was well and truly in the doldrums. In addition to this there are a number of witness accounts confirming the day that

Barbara McNair turned up with the Mafia - she was a lady who had strong mob connections after marrying her Mafia husband - to have a look around Hitsville. I mean, it was a fact that they controlled so much of Detroit, so one little record company could not have prevented any problems if the Mafia chose to take it over. What is a proven fact is that when two shady brothers, attorney Harry Kovick and accountant Sidney Kovick, turned up at Hitsville, as they did regularly, their presence put everybody on edge.

Although I could find no crystal clear evidence that they worked for the Mafia, I did dig up some information that the Kovicks took care of the books, making sure everything finance related was running smoothly. If a Mafia controlled interest had more outgoing than incoming, then the Kovicks would turn up demanding an answer. To look at them, two respectable businessmen posing with Berry Gordy for the camera, they didn't look anything like Mafia men; but what did your ideal Mafia man look like back then? For my take on the question "Did Berry Gordy take out a loan?" I would say that if he did, then he used it to create some brilliant music for the world instead of going into the murky world of Mafia crime.

Did Gordy amass over sixty million dollars in just a few short years, as well as buying the Motown mansion for over a million, by fair means or foul, when he was often seen being driven about with two bodyguards by his side? Enter Edward "Big Foot" Wingate, the owner of the Twenty Grand club, which Gordy used to often frequent searching for new talent. He happened to be Gordy's biggest rival and was the owner of the established record label Golden World Records, which made him one of the most successful businessmen in Detroit. He also owned various properties, ran his own motel and a taxi company, along with several cafes.

The heavy cost of promoting Smokey Robinson and the Miracles had put a serious dent in Berry Gordy's wallet, despite the Miracles handing him the label's first ever million selling single. To save the ship from sinking he spoke to Wingate about becoming a partner in Motown, but Wingate declined his offer in favour of chasing his own dreams of making Golden World Records even more successful than his rivals. A battle slowly began between them as Wingate had his first successful release, a single by the Reflections called 'Just Like Romeo and Juliet', which was followed up by Carl Carlton's 'Nothin Too Sweeter Than Love'. Ed Wingate was well on his way to putting Gordy out of business, moving into a larger, more impressive recording studio in 1965, where he managed to acquire the services of Motown's Funk Brothers to record in his studio, all behind Gordy,s back; he was also re-energising life into his second label, Ric Tic Records.

Apart from his music business, Wingate had other lucrative shady interests, earning him a reputation as one of Detroit's most public criminal figures, and he was watched closely by the police and the FBI. He was Mafia backed and was into gambling, drug dealing and intimidation. There was no better time in Motown's history to join in with the Mafia, guaranteeing Motown's success, but we'll never know. Gordy and Wingate became quite close, and were often seen out and about together in the bars and clubs; and it was this friendship that got Gordy noticed by the police and FBI. However, they couldn't find a speck of evidence connecting him to anything illegal. I'm convinced that the FBI investigations on Gordy were fuelled by racism: they were mesmerised by a black guy who could be so successful and amass so much money in such a short time legally. He was black, therefore he had to have acquired it illegally in a place where few African Americans could ever hope to be successful without help from the Mafia. Clearly Gordy was also a victim of guilt by association. Over the decades it's been common knowledge that celebrities, music stars and wealthy socialites out for kicks have loved to be seen in the company of gangsters; photos are snapped of them shaking hands, kissing, patting each other on the back, hoping to be featured in the morning papers.

Several well-known actors in Hollywood had once been gangsters, like George Raft, before moving on to a safer popular career on the big screen. The antics of the Rat Pack in Vegas hanging out with the town's most dangerous are legendary, and the question everybody wanted answering was whether Old Blue Eyes really was in the Mafia. Not to mention our own fun-loving London gangsters Ronnie and Reg Kray, two of the most feared psychopaths going. They bought a Knightsbridge nightclub called Esmeralda's Barn from where they courted London's social elite like Lucien Freud, Francis Bacon, Barbara Windsor and the Tory MP Lord Boothby, who they exposed as a raging homosexual; all of these flocked to the club to get a taste of life on the dark side. Even Judy Garland, who the twins adored, appeared at the club during a sad downward spiral in her life. Desperate to revive her career, she sadly died a broken spectre of her former self in June 1969 in Cadogan Lane Belgravia after swallowing a massive overdose.

Ed Wingate went on to be even more successful thanks to his new artist Edwin Starr, who handed him a R and B chart entry with the classic 'Agent OO Soul', which was followed by 'Backstreet' and 'SOS – Stop Her On Sight' on his Ric Tic label. Edwin Starr was the artist Berry Gordy had been eyeing up for quite some time before moving in on Wingate for the kill, perhaps the reason being that he'd used Motown's own Funk Brothers for his own purposes behind Gordy's back. He bought out Wingate lock, stock and barrel in 1966, and finished him off later by buying Ric Tic Records and Edwin Starr, firmly establishing

Tamla Motown as Detroit's number one label. Mafia loan or no Mafia loan, that is the question, as Ed Big Foot Wingate sold up and headed for Las Vegas, never to step foot in Detroit again.

THE DEMISE OF DETROIT

Once the fourth biggest city in America, and managing to hold on to that position for several decades, Detroit offered big hopes and dreams to the many thousands of migrant workers arriving at the vast Michigan Central Station looking for work and somewhere to live. It was the production centre for the mighty US automobile industry (Packard, Studebaker, Ford, Chrysler and Hudson) which employed thousands of workers in vast factories so big that they were almost cities within a city. The Fisher Plant, the Hudson Plant, the Ford Piquette Plant, the Highland Park Plant, the Chrysler Axle Plant and the Packard Plant, each boasting state of the art machinery with the capability of producing cars from the factory to the showroom floor in record time. But now they are decaying carcasses, creating an eerie post-apocalyptic Chernobyl-like landscape; huge concrete gravestones in memory of the old US car production industry now inhabited by the homeless, graffiti artists, skateboarders and criminals.

The work was long and arduous, but the wages were good, allowing people to earn decent money to feed and accommodate themselves and their families. The Japanese attack on Pearl Harbour changed everything as suddenly the factories shifted from automobile to arms production on an even more vast scale. In a short period of time some two hundred thousand men enlisted for Uncle Sam, leaving a massive hole in the production force which was first filled by women and then gradually by an army of some three hundred and fifty thousand migrant workers from Europe and across America, who arrived to meet the constant rapid production demands. No other city contributed as much to the war effort as Detroit did, so much so that the city became known as The Arsenal of Democracy. Over ninety percent of steel helmets were produced there, as well as half the number of tanks used, and it is reputed that a complete B24 bomber was built there every hour. Normally only employed to undertake the most dangerous factory jobs, thousands of African Americans now stood shoulder to shoulder with their fellow white workers on the production line in a unified show of strength.

During this time black American workers were treated as less than second class, good enough to work for the war effort with little benefit in return. As more and more of them arrived they were placed in the housing projects called Brewster Douglas and the Sojourner Truth. These were the government's cheap solution to overcrowding, which sprang up in several cities across America. The former was situated in the black neighbourhood of Hastings Street on the edge of the city, comprising four giant tower blocks and other housing which was essentially the deformed offspring of the marriage between wealthy developers out to make more money and architects determined to make a name for themselves at the people's expense. Of course it was built with good intentions, but as is often the case when you build them high and stack them in tight in such a small space in the middle of nowhere, using substandard building materials and builders who couldn't care less about what they were building, things soon started to decay.

Designed as the acceptable affordable blueprint of urban housing schemes the Brewster Douglas project was built to house anywhere between eight to ten thousand people, in a complex featuring rows of ground floor houses and the four giant towers. There was a lot of opposition from many black families, who hated the thought of living in such isolated ghettos, but black protests carried little weight in the thirties and forties and so against their will they moved in. They were subjected to rigorous rules allowing them to live in the projects. The family became the number one priority; the men had to hold down a job and a minimum wage was introduced. When the unexpected happened and Detroit gradually fell into decline, large numbers of properties stood vacant, allowing the chance for African Americans to move in as more and more whites packed up their belongings and moved to the suburbs only a short drive from the city centre. For the council the situation was financially dire as they were unable to charge rents for empty properties which were slowly falling into disrepair, and so they relaxed the once strict rules applying to the residents of Brewster Douglas. It was a move that in reality sounded the death knoll for the project, as crime, violence and drugs became a way of life for many. People began stripping out vacant houses and apartments as the drug dealers occupied the towers, providing themselves with a glorious vantage point from which they could ply their trade in relative comfort.

Black Americans also had to face the constant inhumanity of having to live with a Berlin style wall, built over two metres high, segregating them from the white community as fears grew that they were taking over Detroit. As was often the case with such places, they soon fell into decline, becoming a haven for violent crime and drug dealing as the residents survived the best way they could amidst all this virulent racism. Finally, after years of heated stalemate debates as to whether or not the projects should undergo modernisation, on September 4th 2013 the demolition teams moved in and one year later the site was completely cleared, leaving only the ghosts of those who once lived there and never made it out; although, incredibly, some did make it out and went on to better things. A number of future Motown stars who actually did the impossible included Diana Ross, Smokey Robinson, Mary Wilson and Florence Ballard, and the acclaimed actress Lily Tomlin.

Released in 1972, in my opinion there is no other song that reflected the hopelessness, despair and day to day danger of life in the ghetto than Bobby Womack's 'Across A Hundred And Tenth Street'. People should be given a pleasant environment in which to live, housing they can feel proud of and safe in, and education to allow them the chance of a better, financially stable life. A car, holidays, marriage and a family of their own, and society benefits all round. People are society's responsibility and vice versa in a perfect world. Failure to do that and society will have a war on its hands that it cannot win. In addition to the growing unrest on the streets, bitter resentment increased between white and black workers who were determined to no longer be treated as second class citizens.

The seething white resentment bubbled over in a factory manufacturing engines for aircraft and boats, where some twenty thousand white workers spontaneously downed tools and walked out of the factory just because a group of black workers were promoted, which was a clearly visible sign from the bosses that they were just as willing, able and skilled to get on with the job as their white co-workers. And so the time bomb was ticking away, waiting to explode, and explode it did, as a riot broke out, lasting from the 20th to the 22nd of June in 1943. Many false rumours of racial violence occurring in both black and white neighbourhoods quickly fanned the flames of hatred as the violence hit Detroit like a whirlwind. Over thirty people were killed, twenty-five of whom were black, reported by eye witnesses who were there to have been murdered by the police. Over four hundred more were injured, once again the majority being black people, as six thousand troops arrived to restore order. The cost of property damage was estimated to be over two million dollars in two intense days of rioting. An official report into the riot concluded that the trouble was started by rampaging residents who lived in Paradise Valley, which was black and arguably the most poverty stricken part of Detroit.

Peace and normality, however fragile, at least appeared to have been restored at the very least for Uncle Sam's sake as once again black people stood shoulder to shoulder with whites on the arms production lines; but deep down some wounds never heal, no matter how long the passing of time, and once again, during a boiling a hot Detroit summer, rioting broke out on Sunday 23rd July 1967. According to the facts, over sixty thousand African Americans were housed in the overcrowded slums of Virginia Park, an area that was policed by a predominantly white police force which the majority of locals viewed as nothing more than a brutal racist army of occupation.

By this time the once mighty American automotive industry was beginning to lay off workers, who had previously assumed they had jobs for life. The decline was due to the fact that it wasn't able to compete with the increasing importation of cheaper, better built European and Japanese marques like Mercedes and Datsun, whose models came with many luxuries as standard. The riot - as riots often do - started off small and spontaneously on Twelfth Street, a popular place where people headed for a night out. A party was being held in an illegal drinking club known to be frequented by active members of the Civil Rights

Movement, who were celebrating the return home of a number of African American Vietnam war vets.

A bottle was thrown, tempers flared, and as if on cue the police arrived and quickly started arresting people. More bottles were thrown, which turned into a shower, and in no time at all the police had a race riot on their hands. The police fled to safety after finding themselves heavily outnumbered. All along Twelfth Street fires broke out and looting occurred; the fire brigade arrived, backed up by more police reinforcements, but both were attacked by the mob as they tried without success to dampen the flames. As the worsening situation spiralled even more out of control, some three hundred state police were sent in to break up the riot, but even their efforts proved ineffective as by then the riot had spread to most parts of Virginia Park. Drastic emergency measures were implemented. Shortly after a state of emergency was declared, and the National Guard was sent in to regain law and order.

On the Sunday night some thousand people were in custody, with five people dead and still no signs of the riot ending. Come the Monday things intensified even more, leaving sixteen people dead with no signs whatsoever of the riot stopping; so as a last gasp measure President Lyndon B Johnson took the extreme step of sending in two thousand paratroopers in armoured vehicles to restore peace. As a result of the violence twenty-two more people were killed until finally, on Thursday 27th July, five days after the riot started, Detroit fell silent, with over seven hundred thousand people arrested and damage to property estimated to be close to fifty million dollars, as well as around five thousand people left homeless.

It's incredible to think that in the heat, violence and madness of the riot, Martha Reeves and the Vandellas were in town to perform a number of home coming shows, to help reconnect with the city that gave them their big break, in the fabulous old Fox Theatre. Midway through the show they had no choice but to stop the concert, asking the people to return to their homes as quickly and safely possible. For the first time since Hitsville had opened for business, the legendary Studio A was cloaked in ominous silence as the riot intensified. Despite the building being so close to the rioting and looting, somehow it miraculously survived unscathed, and at the time had eight hit singles in the *Billboard* Hot 100. Otis Williams, one of the Temptations, claimed that he heard the sound of a fifty calibre heavy machine gun not far from where he lived and nobody was more surprised than him to discover Hitsville had come through the riot intact.

God knows what the young budding Motown singer Chris Clark thought as she watched the city burning from the window of the aircraft she was travelling in, along with a number of other artists who'd made the decision to move closer to Hitsville. She recalls a memory from that terrible time of some Motown people fleeing the building carrying as many master tapes as they could in order to save the recordings at all costs. The riot was a pivotal moment in the history of the record label. It was out with the old and in with the new to a large extent, as the music changed a lot, reflecting the political and social change occurring in America, fuelled by the Vietnam war; in words from Edwin Starr and Marvin Gaye people wondered if there would ever come a time once again when there would be dancing in the street.

Detroit's Twelfth Street riot was the third worst in US history, and because of this the President set up the Kerner Commission to investigate the reasons behind the increasing incidents of social unrest taking place across America. The facts were damning to say the least. Between the years of 1965 and 1968, more than one hundred and fifty riots took place, with over eighty people killed in one year alone and one thousand eight hundred injured, along with damage to property amounting to a staggering one hundred million dollars, leaving the Commission to issue the following statement: "Our nation is moving towards two societies - one black - one white - separate and unequal. Discrimination and segregation have long permeated much of American life. They now threaten the future of every American. This deepening racial division is not inevitable. The movement apart can be reversed." It was a clear message back then that black lives mattered with no justice for those responsible for their deaths.

Many people who were there at the time claim that the 1967 Detroit race riots were the beginning of the end for this once thriving industrial metropolis, which once danced to the Motown sound; and for Berry Gordy, more bad news was coming his way. The news was that Holland Dozier Holland, his legendary songwriters, responsible for over two hundred songs including twenty-five number ones, were quitting Motown. Was it any wonder that after living through the riots and then suffering such a damaging loss Gordy decided he couldn't take any more? In June 1972 he took the decision to close down Hitsville, which had remained open for business almost twenty-four seven for thirteen years.

All things considered it seemed like these were perfectly understandable reasons to justify such an action and move to LA - and, as they say, a change is as good as a rest - but there is clear evidence on offer pointing to the fact that the move to LA was anything but spontaneous. It looks more like a well planned eventuality, the planning beginning as early as 1963, when Gordy opened the LA Motown office, not to mention the fact that he stated his intention to move in his announcement in the Central Plaza hotel on the night the Supremes changed their name to Diana Ross and the Supremes. As more and more people left the city responsible for turning Tamla Motown into a successful worldwide multi-million dollar success, there have been several suggestions over the years as to what might have happened to Detroit if Gordy had decided to stay in the city from which so much home grown talent had now become superstars.

As a result of the riot, the government came down heavy on Detroit, greatly reducing all funding to maintain stability, growth, jobs, businesses and education and effectively turning it into a ghost city, where only the bravest and most foolhardy remained in the once great city. Now a person could purchase a house for less than five hundred dollars. With Gordy's growing interest in establishing a film and television company, with made to measure film sets, he could have provided just what Detroit needed, creating crucial jobs and decent wages as well as founding a brand new industry and attracting growth and stability. He could have convinced people not to leave and to give the city a second chance. What if?

One year later, despite keeping his Detroit connection, Gordy and his family moved into their new Californian home. He also rented a house there for Diana Ross and began planning a possible new business opportunity of breaking into the world of television and theatre, no doubt with Diana Ross in mind. Armed with fifteen million dollars he wasted no time in launching Motown Productions, beginning with a special television appearance by Diana Ross under the name *Diana*, quickly followed by featuring her in the film *Lady Sings the Blues* highlighting the career of the brilliant Billie Holliday. It was after the move to LA that the long standing obsession Gordy had for Diana Ross finally ended as she married music manager Robert Silberstein, taking Gordy's biological daughter Rhonda with her. It was an obsession that many blame for the loss of Tamla Motown.

Feelings between Gordy and a number of his most loyal musicians ran high. Funk Brothers guitarist Eddie Willis claimed in an interview that one morning he arrived for work as usual to be greeted by a sign pinned to the door proclaiming "There won't be any work here today." This was followed by more bad news for some three hundred former Motown employees: they were made jobless without ever being given the chance to relocate to LA, as the Tamla Motown empire slowly began to crumble. The Four Tops resigned, followed by the Marvelettes and Martha Reeves, who sang their final emotional goodbye to their beloved Detroit in the Cobo Hall in 1972.

Although far from being as cohesive and productive as it was back in Detroit, business for Gordy continued, albeit minus many of the original artists and musicians who had sweated blood and tears to make Motown successful. From the classic Motown sound, after the move to LA the music changed drastically with the likes of Lionel Ritchie and the Commodores, Tina Marie, Jose Feliciano and De Barge the new future Motown stars. Financial losses soon started to plague Gordy, to the point where the damage was irreversible and he sold the company in 1988 to MCA records for sixty-one million dollars, continuing to operate under various labels like Universal, Island, Def Jam Music Group and Capitol. In 2018 Tamla Motown celebrated its continued existence by releasing a series of compilation albums culled from its extensive back catalogue.

I believe that Detroit's demise was due to a combination of continual long term racial problems and the government cancelling the vital funding that it badly needed for its regeneration after the 1967 riot. Let's not forget that Detroit was the city that had contributed towards winning the Second World War more than any other in America. It deserved infinitely more respect and support than it got; but all is not lost. After years of decay and poverty, the once great city of Detroit is rising from the ashes thanks to some dedicated people determined to rebuild the city they love and call home. Jack White, the musician from the White Stripes, was born and lives in Detroit, and bought the largest masonic temple in the world, which also served as a theatre. He paid off all the back taxes totalling up to some one hundred and forty-three thousand dollars, purely on a sentimental whim because his mother once worked there as an usherette, and to honour his gesture, the council renamed it the Jack White Theatre.

A group of hardened dedicated Model T car fanatics have formed the Model T Automotive Heritage Complex, buying areas of the original Ford Piquette Avenue plant where thousands of Model Ts rolled off the production line. The grand Michigan Central Station has been bought by the Ford motor company with plans to convert it into a mixed facility. Their plan is to be a part of Detroit once again with a one million two hundred thousand square foot centre developing electrical vehicles and urban services thanks to a massive investment of seven hundred and forty million dollars.

And the former photographic studio on 2648 West Boulevard is still there, the place that was renamed Hitsville USA, the first home and what many agree is the only home of the legendary Tamla Motown label founded by Berry Gordy in 1959. His grand Italian style ten bedroomed mansion remains the same, looking much as it did when he purchased it, situated on the exclusive West Boston Boulevard in the city's historical Edison district, where some of the Motown stars performed. And the fabulous Fox Theatre is once again open for business, where Martha Reeves and her Vandellas once performed in the city they loved during a terrible time that changed Detroit, but not forever.

MY MOTOWN ARTISTS

Aretha Franklin – Otis Redding – Ray Charles – Rufus Thomas – The Drifters – Don Covay – Wilson Pickett – Percy Sledge – Sam and Dave – The Bar-Kays – Eddie Floyd – Arthur Conley – William Bell – Donny Hathaway – Carla Thomas – Booker T and the MG´S – Dorothy Moore – Freda Payne – Inez and Charlie Foxx – Major Lance – Mel and Tim – The Dramatics – The Delphonics. The above artists from the Atlantic and Stax record labels, who many times intermingled from label to label including Motown, represent some of the greatest soul artists of their day. To me good soul music is exactly that, and after I first discovered it, I collected many singles recorded on Stax and Atlantic.

As good as they were - and they were good - they lacked that indefinable, instantly recognisable magical something that the Tamla Motown artists had in abundance, the sound that the Funk Brothers created in that cramped studio in Hitsville USA as if you could hear just about everything that was going on in that confined space. The unique bass lines driving everything along, the horns in all the right places, the unique drum rolls and the keyboard filling in the rest in tune with whatever artist happened to be recording at the same time created what for me was addictive danceable music.

In the Blackpool nightclubs of the 70s, the different styles of music had their own pecking order on the dancefloor, their own fifteen minutes of fame so to speak. Hippies would hit the floor, baubles, bangles and beads, long hair loons and Afghan coats, weaving and swaying to Jethro Tull and Cat Stevens. Rockers were up next with their long hair and leathers, thumbs tucked into the waistbands of their jeans, tearing it up to Status Quo and Motorhead. Elegant Roxy Music lounge lizards took over, clicking their fingers and moving from side to side trying to emulate Bryan Ferry, singing along to 'Virginia Plain', 'Love Is The Drug' or 'Do The Strand'. Seconds after that the club exploded to Sweet's 'Ballroom Blitz', and glam rockers would pile on the floor in their satin and glitter clothes followed by the Bowie freaks in their suits and make up attempting to mime dance to 'John I'm Only Dancing' or 'Panic In Detroit' and taking themselves far too seriously.

As soon as Bowie ended the disco crowd would be up, doing their best 'Saturday Night Fever', the girls looking sexy and the guys wearing white suits and shirts unbuttoned to the waist; and then it was the turn of the soul crowd. Boys and girls slipping and sliding across the floor, effortlessly in tune with the music as if they were gliding on air. Looking sharp in Ben Sherman and Brutus shirts, Fred Perry polo shirts, suits, and polished leather soled brogues and loafers. It was a curious musical symbiosis that seemed to work in the clubs until the holidaymakers appeared and the booze kicked in as the lights went on, the music stopped and another night ended in chaos. Soul music has been with me in its various genres for the greater part of my life, from teenager to adult, like a long standing marriage faced with the occasional ups and downs that always occur during the low times, when familiarity breeds mistaken contempt, followed by a consultation with the wedding counsellor to help us revisit and rediscover the original reasons why we fell in love in the first place so that flame can be reignited over again.

To be brutally honest, apart from a few notable exceptions, I was never into Tamla Motown and the music it produced when it moved from Detroit to Los Angeles. Apart from 'Uptight', 'Superstition' and 'Living In The City', Stevie Wonder's later recordings did nothing for me. And as much as his talent is indisputable and there will never ever be another Michael Jackson, I didn't like his music, especially his early recordings like 'Rocking Robin' and 'Ben'. And I never saw eye to eye with Lionel Ritchie, Boyz To Men, The Pointer Sisters and Tony Braxton. For me the original infectious, relentless, soulful driving beat of Detroit Tamla Motown died the day Berry Gordy moved the label to Los Angeles, despite Smokey Robinson's statement that Motown always captured that unique sound wherever the artists recorded. At the time Detroit was a thriving industrial city, not without its fair share of simmering racial and social problems that many Motown artists lived with on a daily basis, not to mention the sinister, frequently violent presence of both the Italian and Black Mafia on the Detroit streets. In my opinion, many of those artists brought their personal experiences to the Hitsville studio, which to me was partly responsible for helping to create the classic Motown sound from 1960 to 1972. It was a sound that was never to be repeated when the city was left to fend for itself.

And so to the question I remember countless people have asked me over the decades whenever the subject of Tamla Motown rises to the conversational fore, and the very same one I've asked myself over the years: just who are my favourite male and female Tamla Motown artists? It's a tough question to answer, and my answer has constantly changed over the years when it comes down to who and who not to leave out. I guess it all comes down to specific tracks I fell in love with back then and still love today, over fifty years later, recorded by artists who walked through the doors of Hitsville USA on a wing and a prayer, hoping to sign a record deal, before Maxine Powell got her hands on them and trained them to look as good as, if not better than, the music they were singing. So here are some of my favourite Motown singles, immortalised by the male and female artists who provided me with so many great memories from my younger years, and made me go out and search for that unique soul sound that made my heart beat and my feet move a hell of a lot faster than they do today - but we all had our day, didn't we?

THE SUPREMES

To this day the Supremes remain America's most successful female vocal group, scoring a dozen number one singles on the *Billboard* Hot 100 and rivalling the Beatles in global popularity back in the day. They were just four ordinary girls with big dreams, who were residents in the dreadful Brewster Douglas housing project, from where few escaped, starting out with all the odds stacked against them of making it as successful artists for Tamla Motown. Diana Ross, Mary Wilson, Florence Ballard and Betty McGlown formed a group called the Primettes and started performing in and around Detroit, and came to the attention of Berry Gordy thanks to Smokey Robinson, who persuaded Gordy to give them an audition. Although he liked them Gordy thought they were far too young, and as was the case with many of his younger stars he suggested they finish off their education before thinking of embarking on a musical career. Their persistence finally paid off, after spending all their spare time after school hanging around Hitsville until somebody took notice of them.

Smokey arranged a second audition for the girls and this time Gordy offered them a recording contract, subject to a change of name - and so the Supremes were born, although Betty McGlown left the group. Their early Motown career started off somewhat disastrously, recording six songs none of which managed to make the charts. Determined to make amends, the Supremes covered as much studio work as they could, singing backing vocals for a number of artists including Marvin Gaye and Smokey Robinson in a serious attempt to perfect their craft; and it paid off. In 1963 the girls hit the *Billboard* Hot 100 with the single 'When The Loving Starts Shining Through'. With Holland Dozier Holland assigned to writing much of their new material, they were only a stone's throw away from success courtesy of singles 'Where Did Our Love Go', 'Baby Love', 'Come See About Me', 'Stop In The Name Of Love', 'You Can't Hurry Love', 'You Keep Me Hanging On' and 'Back In My Arms Again'.

These singles became massive international hits just at the time when Berry Gordy started to focus his attention on the young Diana Ross, developing a lifelong obsession with the singer. To advance her career sadly the Supremes became Diana Ross and the Supremes, and although they continued to be successful, the new change of name didn't sit too easily with Florence Ballard and Mary Wilson, and indirectly signalled the end of the Supremes as the world knew them. Increasing arguments between the girls and Motown artists who thought that Gordy was paying far too much attention to Diana Ross added more problems for the trio. Florence Ballard took things really badly, suffering depression and heavy drinking, and she eventually left the Supremes of her own accord rather than face the humiliation of being sacked by Berry Gordy. Her departure was followed by Mary Wilson.

The Supremes were nominated for a Grammy Award for Best Rhythm and Blues Recording for 'Baby Love', Best Rhythm and Blues Vocal Performance for 'Stop In The Name of Love', the Grammy Hall of Fame for 'Where Did Our Love Go', 'You Keep Me Hanging On' and 'Stop In The Name of Love'. The original line up was inducted into the Rock and Roll Hall of Fame in 1968 and awarded a star on the Hollywood Hall of Fame in 1994 - and it didn't stop there. In 2004 *Rolling Stone* magazine voted them ninety-seven on their One Hundred Greatest Artists of All Time list. Fitting lasting tributes for three former young girls from the wrong side of the tracks who made the big time, the Supremes really did live up to their name and then some.

DIANA ROSS (SOLO CAREER)

Celebrating a truly incredible music career spanning five decades, it would be easier to list the awards Diana Ross hasn't received. She was nominated thirteen times for the Grammy Awards between 1965 and 1983, and awarded a Lifetime Achievement Award in 2012. Diana Ross won six out of nine American Music Awards, the MTV Music Video Award in 1985 for the single 'We Are The World', 1973 Academy Award for the film *Lady Sings The Blues*, the 1973 *Cue* magazine award for Entertainer of the Year, 1973 Golden Globe Award for the most promising female newcomer, 1976 *Billboard* award for Female Entertainer of the Year, 1977 Tony Award for the acclaimed *An Evening With Diana Ross*, 1982 a star in the Hollywood Walk of Fame, 1993 *Guinness Book of Records* award for the most successful singer of all time, 1994 Diana Ross and The Supremes awarded a star in the Hollywood Walk of Fame, 1995 the Soul Train Music Awards, 1996 *Billboard* Entertainer of the Century, 1996 inducted into the Soul Train Hall of Fame, 1998 inducted into the Songwriters Hall of Fame, 1999 inducted into the National Academy of Recording Arts and Sciences, 2007 the BET Music Awards Lifetime Achievement Award, 2012 Grammy Award, 2016 awarded the Presidential Medal of Freedom, and 2017 the American Music Awards Lifetime Achievement Award.

Diana Ross is without doubt an artist of immense talent, but even now, people who were there in Hitsville back in the day still question if she'd have got to where she is without Berry Gordy moulding her for the world of superstardom. Either way you cannot dispute the fact that the young girl with a dream of becoming a singer trapped in the hopelessness of the Detroit Housing Projects has done exceedingly well for herself. After quitting the Supremes in 1970 Diana Ross's solo live shows were greeted with critical acclaim and *Variety* magazine went further by saying "she is a total entertainer." Her first successful solo single was the classic 'Ain't No Mountain High Enough' and there really wasn't a mountain high enough as Diana Ross climbed the staircase to global superstardom.

Thanks to Berry Gordy's unswerving belief in her, Hollywood beckoned, and Diana answered the call starring as Billie Holliday in the acclaimed movie *Lady Sings The Blues*, which earned her an Oscar nomination for the Best New Actress. Two years later she was back on the silver screen starring in *Mahogany* and had a number one hit with the film's theme tune, 'Do You Know Where You're Going To'. This was followed a year later with the moving ballad 'Touch Me In The Morning'. The crowds flocked to her sell out shows as Diana Ross summed up the reason why she enjoyed performing so much: "It doesn't matter if I'm in a stadium filled with thousands of people or in a much smaller venue. My interaction with the audience is always on a one to one basis."

Her incredible musical legacy includes twenty-four studio albums from 1970 to 2006, five film soundtracks and five live albums. At the age of seventy-six, Diana Ross was about to embark on a UK tour in 2020 ending with a show at the Sunday Afternoon Legends slot at Glastonbury to help celebrate the festival's fiftieth anniversary; but everything is on hold until the world is rid of the curse of the coronavirus.

MARTHA REEVES AND THE VANDELLAS

The soulful stomping sound of 'Nowhere To Run' by the one and only Martha Reeves and her Vandellas can still turn up the heat on my thinning blood, transporting me back to happier youthful times, but it was their first single, before the Supremes, that really helped to establish them within the Motown empire. They released 'Heatwave' in 1963. The single reached the number one spot in the *Billboard* Hot R and B chart as well as number four in the Hot 100, their sound being described as "the young sound of America". Their musical origins are almost a mirror image of how the Supremes got together and performed on the Detroit club circuit.

The group came together in 1957, started by close friends Annette Beard, Rosalind Ashford, and Gloria Williams, who were later joined by Alabama born Martha Reeves. At this time she was already chiselling out a solo career in Detroit, where she was spotted by Motown's talent spotter Mickey Stevenson, who was hoping to discover the next big success. Martha originally worked as Mickey's secretary in Hitsville, arranging various auditions and befriending many of the artists who were coming and going. Originally calling themselves the Vels, the girls found themselves providing backing vocals on Marvin Gaye's first single 'Stubborn Kind Of Fellow'. As luck would have it their first demo recording 'I'll Have To Let Him Go' somehow found its way into Gordy's finely tuned ears and he offered them a record contract, largely because of the fact that he was so impressed with Martha Reeves' voice.

This important time in the group's artistic development sadly signalled the departure of one of the founder members, Gloria Williams, who suddenly lost her appetite for the showbiz world, preferring the quieter life of listening to music as opposed to performing it. As was the case with the Supremes, Martha decided to change the group's name, and they called themselves the Vandellas. At the time Martha lived close to Van Street Detroit, a neighbourhood separating blacks from the whites. Her idol was the singer Della Reese so she put the two together, coming up with Van - Della; and once again another Hitsville legend was born. Their single successes included 'Come And Get These Memories', 'Heatwave', 'Quicksand', 'Nowhere To Run', 'Jimmy Mack' , 'Bless You' and the massively popular 'Dancing In The Street', later performed magnificently by David Bowie and Mick Jagger in what to me became the signature tune for Live Aid, and a song which, along with 'Heatwave', was inducted into the Grammy Hall of Fame, as well as being named in the Rock and Roll Hall of Fame as one of the songs that helped shape rock and roll.

Martha Reeves and the Vandellas enjoyed more recognition of their music in 1995 when they were inducted into the Rock and Roll Hall of Fame, being one of only two female groups to be awarded the honour, followed by their induction into the Vocal Group Hall of Fame in 2003 and a Grammy Award nomination for Best R and B Performance for their hit 'Heatwave'. In 2006 'Dancing In The Street' was included in the United States Library of Congress

National Recording Registry in recognition of its massive artistic, historical and cultural significance.

Just as Barbara McNair experienced the ugly face of racism prevalent in many US states during a time in America when black Americans were treated as less than second class citizens, so too did Martha and her Vandellas, as she once recalled with a certain grace and dignity: "When we played in the south, we were not allowed to sit at the main counter in the restaurants we ate in. The staff served us up cold coffee, hot dogs and hamburgers and we were even forced to drink water from public fountains with Blacks Only written on them. We even experienced people shooting at us under the assumption that we were going to do more harm than good but I'm glad we went through all that because we made it possible for other artists to tour later on."

And what of the many rumours of the bitter feud that supposedly went on between Diana Ross and herself? She dismissed them outright, leaving those who were there at the time to make their own minds up. "There might have been a confrontation over some costumes but Diana and I were never rivals. They were there at Motown before us but it took them longer to break through. They were desperate for a hit but failed to reach the charts at first. Then Berry got Holland Dozier Holland to write 'Where Did Our Love Go' for them and after that they had five number ones in a row. They were good but we were good too. Our sound was different whereas theirs had the same beat but people liked them. I learnt how to be a one take artist at Motown. If you didn't crack a song by the second take there would be someone waiting outside the door to take your place." Wise cutting words spoken by the mighty Martha Reeves reflecting on the intense competition that went on behind the doors of Hitsville USA, which certainly practised a strict do or die policy to bring out the very best of the label's artists in the shortest possible time.

KIM WESTON

'Take Me In Your Arms' was another class Motown monster courtesy of Holland Dozier Holland, sung by another of my favourite artists, Kim Weston, who was born in 1939 and first signed with Motown in 1961, having been a member of a popular Detroit gospel group called Wright Special. She was chosen to work with songwriter Norman Whitfield, but her stay was short lived and she left the label three years later despite working with Smokey Robinson. Two years after signing she had her first real chart success with a single called 'It Should Have Been Me', together with a B-side called 'Love Me All The Way' that proved to be much more popular than the A-side. With this in mind Motown re-released it as an A-side and it made number twenty-four on the R and B charts and number eighty-eight on the Pop chart.

Marvin Gaye needed a partner to work with on a number of duets in the planning and so Kim was brought back to Motown to record a track called 'What Good Am I Without You', which only managed to reach twenty-five on the R and B chart and an even worse sixty-one on the Pop charts. It was a clear indication that Kim badly needed a change in direction if she was going to remain with Motown, so she began working with Holland Dozier Holland and recorded the classic 'Take Me In Your Arms' single that became her biggest hit of the time. Kim's vocal talents were ideally suited to soft ballads but Eddie Holland saw something in her that she clearly missed, as he recalled later: " 'Take Me In Your Arms' was raunchy and Kim had one of those voices I thought was very powerful." Holland's efforts were amply rewarded as the single rocketed to number four in the R and B chart and fifty in the Pop chart.

Kim married Motown A and R chief Mickey Stevenson, who took on the challenge of providing her with the kind of success other Motown artists enjoyed, but for her sadly the marriage with Tamla Motown didn't work out the way she had hoped and in 1966 the two parted amicably as Kim followed her husband to MGM records. In August of the same year fate stepped in, in the kind of weird and wonderful way it often does, instigated by Gordy, who released an album called *It Takes Two* comprising a compilation of duets performed by Kim and Marvin Gaye. The album was a success, with the title track doing so well it hit number four in the R and B chart and fourteen in the Pop chart, providing both artists with their first real big success in Europe, though this was followed by bitter disappointment at not being allowed to perform the song together because Kim was no longer a signed Motown artist.

Kim moved to Stax records in 1971, where she recorded a succession of singles that never really equalled the success of 'It Takes Two', her only recording fame during that time being a critically acclaimed performance in the LA Coliseum where she sang 'Lift Every Voice And Sing' to a packed audience. For Kim unexpected fate was waiting to bring her more success: in the 1970s in the UK the northern soul scene had exploded, inspiring DJ and record producer Ian Levine to release a selection of Kim's classic Tamla Motown tracks, including 'It Takes Two', which she recorded with the brother of Marvin Gaye,

Frankie, plus an album called *Investigate*. But her biggest UK success was the single that endeared her to the hearts of northern soul fans on the scene across the country, her single 'Helpless'; from the second she starts singing, I join her on her heartbroken walk down a loveless street searching for love and romance and it's a record that is still one of the best ever, and still sends that shiver down my spine that only the very best of the best singles manage to do.

A few years ago I enjoyed a fleeting moment when she, Kim Weston, appeared in the entertainment suite of Blackpool Football Club; I was standing by the exit enjoying a breather as she glided into the room, and for a woman in her seventies, she still looked sensational. She was dressed in a white trouser suit and a long fur coat and her hair and make up were immaculate, and since she was clearly in the mood for meeting people I walked over to say hello. "Oh yeah hi Ms Weston, it's a privilege and an honour to meet you," was the line I originally planned to say but God knows how many times she must have heard that old predictable chestnut so I simply settled for a brief "Hi Ms Weston, glad to meet you." She is a lady who still carries on the legacy she learned in the Maxine Powell Finishing School and adamantly refuses to allow the reality of time passing her by - and why should she? Kim Weston was inducted into the official R and B Hall of Fame in August 2013 in recognition of her contribution to the music industry - well deserved to a true lady of soul music.

BRENDA HOLLOWAY

Brenda Holloway's 'Just Look What You Done' from beginning to end just oozes all the hallmarks of classic Motown from an even classier lady. Born in Atascadero California in 1946 and raised in the Watts Housing Project, Brenda originally hailed from a classical music background but her model looks and versatile voice soon brought her to the attention of Berry Gordy. He wasted no time at all in offering the young seventeen-year-old a record contract, convinced that she had the talent to go all the way. As she was from Los Angeles, she was offered the chance to record in the Motown studio, where she was introduced to Hal Davis and Marc Gordon who were responsible for her first successful recording. This was a soulful ballad called 'Every Little Bit Hurts' that suited her vocal range perfectly.

Despite her having some serious doubts about the song, it was released in 1964 and hit the number thirteen spot on the *Billboard* Hot 100 which in turn earned her a place on the UK bound Tamla Motown Soul Revue in 1965. Following the surprising departure of Mary Wells from the Motown stable, Brenda stepped into her shoes and recorded a number of songs composed by Smokey Robinson including the hit single 'When I'm Gone', which hit number twenty-five on the Hot 100 as well as the thirteenth spot on the R and B chart. This was followed by a single called 'Operator', but that failed to come close to her earlier material as Brenda hit some unexpected problems.

One of only a few artists who flatly refused to attend Maxine Powell's finishing school, during a number of recording sessions in Hitsville many of the songwriters and musicians working with her confirmed that she was turning out to be somewhat of an argumentative, temperamental troublemaker. As a result of her behaviour, focus was quickly shifted to some of Motown's more successful, easier going artists, and Brenda found herself forced out of the spotlight. Her one big highlight during this troubled time was that she actually toured with the Beatles in 1965, the recorded shows opening a new door for her as a television celebrity.

In addition to this new found opportunity, more recording success followed in 1967 with her classic single 'Just Look What You've Done', which took the number twenty-one spot on the R and B chart and was quickly followed by 'You've Made Me So Very Happy', a song co-written by her sister Patrice, which reached number thirty-nine on the Hot 100 and forty on the R and B chart. Despite this success, Brenda Holloway and Tamla Motown parted company in 1968 due to some unresolved problems, after which she recorded some new songs with Holland Dozier Holland for the Invictus and Music Merchant labels, as well as securing a tour with Joe Cocker doing backing vocals. She also flirted with gospel music, recording an album that never hit the intended mark.

Following Kim Weston's good fortune, Brenda Holloway found similar unexpected success on the UK northern soul scene thanks to Ian Levine's record label Motor City Records, where some of her songs have become popular soul anthems to this day. In 1999 she was honoured with the Rhythm and Blues Foundation's prestigious

Pioneer Award and she continues today as a performing artist, celebrating a successful career in the music industry for over fifty years. She is a lady who will be linked forever more to those early Tamla Motown days.

THE VELVELETTES

Out of all of the Tamla Motown hierarchy that never achieved the success they should have, the Velvelettes stand out. They came together in 1961, originally a five girl group comprising cousins Bertha and Norma Barbe, sisters Mildred and Caroline Gil, and friend Betty Kelly. The first taste of their potential musical career occurred when they travelled to Kalamazoo performing in and successfully winning a talent contest and the princely sum of twenty-five dollars. A second opportunity came along when two of them met a friend at university who just happened to know Berry Gordy, who arranged for them to meet him. Waiting for them was Motown A and R man Micky Stevenson, who gave the girls an audition, their sweet soul harmonies impressing him so much that he immediately signed them up. They were handed two singles, 'There He Goes' and 'That's The Reason Why', featuring Stevie Wonder on Harmonica. These were followed by their first public show in Detroit, in a competition between a number of Motown stars at the fabulous Greystone ballroom, where they went head to head with the mighty Diana Ross and the Supremes. The Velvelettes went down exceptionally well with the audience and the Supremes left with their tails between their dresses.

1964 saw them recording with Norman Whitfield, who handed them the single 'Needle In A Haystack', which became their biggest career success. Then Betty left when she heard there was a place on offer with Martha Reeves and the Vandellas, and Mildred left the group to look after her newborn baby. Two more successful singles followed, 'He's So Fine' and 'He Was Really Saying Something', which claimed the number sixty-four spot on the Pop chart and twenty-one on the R and B chart. Just at the time they appeared to be be on the verge of the kind of success they'd been wanting, via tours and various television appearances, the group went their separate ways for personal reasons. In later years though the five of them met up to perform a show, and after enjoying the feeling of being back on stage they have continued, touring even now, holding the record for the only Motown group performing with the original members - and that's got to be worth celebrating.

THE MARVELETTES

The Marvelettes' 'Destination Anywhere' is an instant finger-clicking toe-tapping song, and who could resist a train journey with one of Tamla Motown's most celebrated female groups? They were responsible for the label's first number one single, 'Please Mister Postman', in 1961 and what finer way to begin a musical career via a succession of talent contests under their original line up: Gladys Horton, Katherine Anderson, Juanita Cowart, Georgeanna Tillman and Georgia Dobbins.

Gordy was impressed by the girls but insisted they had to get back to him with a hit single, so they set to work with a friend, William Garrett, to write 'Please Mister Postman'. It took only fifteen weeks to hit the number one spot on the *Billboard* Hot 100, an incredible musical debut quickly followed up by two more hits, 'Playboy' and 'Beechwood', penned by Marvin Gaye. Gordy took the decision to strip them down to a trio, which meant saying goodbye to Georgeanna Tillman and Juanita Cowart. The all new line up continued to work with Smokey Robinson, who wrote their next hits 'As Long As I Know He's Mine' and 'He's A Good Guy'.

Then in 1965 Wanda Royers was brought in as lead vocalist, thanks to the connection of her being the wife of

Miracles artist Bobby Royers, and the new change proved to be successful. The single 'I'll Keep Holding On' reached the thirty-four spot on the Rhythm and Blues chart and was followed by 'Danger Heartbreak Dead Ahead', which claimed the number eleven spot, and a Smokey Robinson song 'Don't Mess With Bill' that reached number seven in the Top Ten. It was the second single to top the one million sales mark. In 1970 - and once again with Smokey's help - they produced the album *Return of the Marvelettes* which featured covers of their greatest hits, but surprisingly the album failed to cut the mustard with no chart singles and only reaching number fifty on the Rhythm and Blues chart. Disenchanted with this the group disbanded and went their separate ways; this was then followed by a legal battle with Motown for non-payment of royalties. Their single 'Only Your Love Can Save Me' became another one of those massive soul anthems played at soul nights across the UK to this day.

In 1995 the Marvelettes were awarded the Pioneer Award at the Rhythm and Blues Foundation. In 2004 they were inducted into the Vocal Group Hall of Fame. In 2005 they were awarded two gold plaques for their million selling singles 'Please Mister Postman' and 'Don't Mess With Bill'. In 2007 they were also voted into the Michigan Rock and Roll Hall of Fame. 2013 saw them as nominations into the Rock and Roll Hall of Fame and after the second attempt they were finally inducted. The same year saw them inducted into the Rhythm and Blues Music Hall of Fame in Cleveland and two years later in Detroit. The writer Susan Whithall once described them as being the archetypal early 1960s college girls, who were wholesome, likeable and cute. Yes, undoubtably they were successful artists, with their biggest single 'Needle In A Haystack' followed by what I consider their equally best single 'He Was Really Saying Something' but sadly, as was the case with a number of

Tamla Motown artists, the Marvelettes never quite achieved the kind of constant success they should have done.

CHRIS CLARK

A truly gifted white artist in the company of black artists, to me Chris Clark was a rare effortless combination of Petula Clark and Dusty Springfield, a tall, gorgeous, silver blonde blue-eyed girl nicknamed the "White Negress" whose storming track 'Love's Gone Bad' combines the influences of Billie Holliday and Etta James. The official Tamla Motown historian once wrote of her: "Chris is the real deal." Chris Clark was born in Santa Cruz California and was still in her teens when LA based Hal Davis sent her off to Hitsville to audition for Berry Gordy. Her moving a capella version of 'All I Could Do Was Cry', a song originally penned by Gordy, secured her a record contract. As was the case with many future stars, Chris began working as a secretary, dreaming of the day when her big chance would come and propel her to fame and fortune.

Her first single 'Do Right Baby Do Right' was released in 1965 and attracted scant success; because of this, Motown delayed her second single 'Do I Love You', although this later became a cult success with record collectors worldwide. Her third release saw Chris Clark signalling her arrival with a bang, a storming, bouncing, organ-orientated soul record called 'Love's Gone Bad' which contains all the essential ingredients that make a soul record great and was penned by Holland Dozier Holland at their very best together. There was also a fabulous version of 'Put Yourself In My Place' on the B-side and it was followed up by an LP. However, despite it being a great album, with one track, 'Sweeter As The Days Go By', that became a big hit in the UK, the album fell short of Motown's expectations.

A change of artistic direction saw Chris working on a screenplay penned by Gordy called *The Lady Sings The Blues,* which was about the life of Billie Holliday. Chris really rose to the challenge by rewriting much of the screenplay dialogue and as a result the film became an acclaimed success, providing the perfect platform to launch Diana Ross's film career, earning an Academy Award Nomination. In 2009 the album *Soul Sounds* was released containing a selection of Chris Clark's unreleased material, after which she ended up as the executive for Tamla Motown's film production division as well as creative assistant on the Hollywood blockbuster *Mahogany,* earning her promotion to head of Motown's creative affairs. Chris Clark lives in Santa Rosa working as a screenwriter, photographer and singer, and her performance in the video of the song 'Ghosts Of San Francisco' won the Mixed Genre Jazz Award at the NYC Jazz Film Festival.

TAMMI TERRELL

Without doubt one of Motown's potential greats, tragically Tammi Terrell was only twenty-four when she died of brain cancer after a long and agonising fight for life. Tammi was born in Philadelphia on the 29th April 1945 to parents Jennie Graham and Thomas Montgomery, with an older sister Ludie, and from an early age she showed she had the talent to go far, so much so that James Brown's own record label, Try Me records, produced her first single 'I Cried', which scraped into the *Billboard* 100 at number ninety-nine. Tammi always felt the need for an education that would provide her with a solid enough foundation to fall back on, so she enrolled at Pennsylvania University for two years despite music remaining very much in her heart.

It was at this time when the established singer, songwriter and musician Jerry Butler pleaded with Tammi to perform a number of shows with him in between continuing with her studies. Once again, as luck would have it, fate stepped in to elevate the young singer to early stardom after a brilliant performance in Detroit's fabulous Twenty Twenty club, where many future Motown stars would perform. No guesses as to who was in the audience - Mister Motown himself, Berry Gordy, who signed her up on April 29th 1965, giving her a fantastic twentieth birthday present. Tammi's original name was a hefty sounding Thomasina Winifred Montgomery, a name that didn't fit in at all with the cool, sharp, slick Motown image, so Gordy abbreviated it down to a more manageable Tammi Terrell.

With a new name in place she hit the R and B Top 40 with a single 'I Can't Believe You Love Me', quickly followed up with a second, 'Come On And See Me'. Tammi was well on her way, recording with the Temptations, Stevie Wonder and the Isley Brothers as well as starring in the Motown Revue, in which she opened the shows alongside the Temptations. As she quickly established herself as a rising star, with a gifted, effortless voice, Gordy teamed her up with Marvin Gaye with the intention of recording several duets they claimed as their own. Their first was the classic 'Ain't No Mountain High Enough', which made it to number nineteen on the *Billboard* Hot 100 and number three on the R and B charts. The duo's second single was 'Your Precious Love', which did even better, hitting the number five spot on the Pop chart and number two on the R and B chart. This was followed by the release of the album *United* which featured a selection of their duets.

The two went on tour with a number of shows, during which she quickly became the mainstay of the duo due to the fact that Marvin Gaye hated performing live. During one of their shows, illness got the better of Tammi, and one night she collapsed in the arms of her closest Motown friend who she shared so much of her success with and who suffered many emotional problems as a result of her untimely death; the only Motown star her mother allowed to her funeral, Gordy included. Tammi Terrell and Marvin Gaye were voted number one in the *Cashbox* magazine yearly survey. An award for the Best Rhythm and Blues Vocal Performance for 'Ain't No Mountain High Enough' at the tenth annual Grammy Awards in 1968 was followed by the song being inducted into the Grammy Hall of Fame in 1999. All in all Tammi left twenty singles and six compilation albums to her name. The late great Tammi Terrell sadly left us at far too young an age; she is impossible to forget and we will always wonder what could have been.

GLORIA JONES

Gloria Jones was born in Cincinnati in 1945, and like so many future Motown artists, she cut her musical teeth in gospel music after her family moved to Los Angeles. Her first group went under the unlikely name of the COGICS - church of God in Christ - actually recording an album on the Vee-Jay label called, appropriately enough, *It's A Blessing*. Gloria's powerful singing style stood out from the rest of the band members, so much so that she attracted the attention of Hal Davis, head of the LA Motown office, who gave her the chance to sing some backing vocals for Brenda Holloway and her sister Patrice. Gloria fitted in like a glove and started writing and arranging songs almost immediately. Her first single was released in 1964, called 'My Bad Boy's Coming Home'. It failed to hit the chart, but all was not lost as the B-side, called 'Tainted Love', became a massive soul anthem in the UK and on the northern soul scene it is still played and loved to this day.

Gloria moved to England and soon became an established member of the song writing team, penning hits for Eddie Kendricks, Diana Ross, Marvin Gaye and the Four Tops. Her album *Share My Love* is widely regarded by many as her finest work; it manages to incorporate many musical styles from soul to flamenco, making it a little known gem of an album. Through her relationship with Marc Bolan, who she later married, Gloria moved to the UK after being offered the chance to join his glam rock band T-Rex, releasing one album called *Vision,* signed to EMI. Sadly tragedy followed when Marc Bolan was killed in a car accident, leaving Gloria to pack up and head back to the States to pick up the pieces of her musical career.

Gloria is still writing and recording and her best album *Share My Love* was re-released by Tamla Motown in 2009. 'Tainted Love', her famous B-side, became a massive worldwide success thanks to UK electro duo Soft Cell's stripped down version, but it's the original that still hits the spot for me, with Gloria's powerful fast vocal range making it one of those instantly recognisable classics.

MARY WELLS

One of the very early original voices of Motown, Mary Wells was born in Detroit in 1943 and from a very early age struggled with ill health; she had spinal meningitis that left her temporarily paralysed and semi-blind at the age of two. Her childhood was poor and tough to say the least, with no father around and a mother who earned low pay working as a domestic, calling on young Mary to help her out as and when needed. Mary was a tough kid who refused to lie down and die and through her passion for singing managed to progress from her love of gospel music to getting bookings in a number of Detroit nightclubs. Mary also dabbled with song writing, with one in particular for Jackie Wilson. After a meeting with Berry Gordy, Mary impressed him enough to actually allow her to go on to record the single 'Bye Bye Baby' which was released in 1960, and nobody was more surprised than her when the news broke that the single had reached the number eight spot on the *Billboard* R and B chart and number forty-five in the Pop chart in 1961.

Now a signed Motown artist, Mary began working with Smokey Robinson on some early material, and in 1962 she hit the number two spot on the R and B chart with the single 'The One Who Really Loves You'. Hot on the heels of that, Mary took the prestigious number two spot on the R and B chart as well as a credible number nine on the Pop chart with another Smokey Robinson song, 'You Beat Me To The Punch'. To all those involved it was crystal clear that Mary was on her way to becoming a Motown superstar, and in 1963 more singles brought her chart successes with 'Laughing Boy', 'Your Old Standby' and 'You Lost The Sweetest Boy'.

The following year saw Motown release what has become her trademark, instantly recognisable worldwide hit 'My Guy' thanks yet again to Smokey Robinson's magical way with words. It took the number one spot on the *Cashbox* R and B chart for seven weeks as well as the R and B single of the year, and gave Mary Wells her second million selling single. 'My Guy' instantly transformed her from a US to an international star and in the UK the easy to listen to single hit the number five spot on the UK pop chart. The Beatles loved the song so much that they invited Mary to join them on their tour, an accolade only previously given to Brenda Holloway and Jackie Deshannon. The incredible success of 'My Guy' was summed up perfectly by Motown's sales chief Barney Ales when he said that he didn't think that there was an audience from thirty to fifty that didn't know the words to 'My Guy'. To me the song epitomised the classic Motown sound that started out life in that cramped Hitsville studio and that took the world by storm and then some.

A bitter lengthy legal battle between Mary and Berry Gordy ensued, with Mary claiming that a large percentage of her owed royalties were being used by Gordy to promote the Supremes, causing her to finally leave Motown in 1965 with a cash award. She then signed for 20th Century Fox Records, who reputedly eased her financial troubles with a hefty two hundred thousand dollar contract. Various singles were released but none were as successful as her previous hits alongside Smokey Robinson. There followed a sad time when her health took a turn for the worse; she contracted tuberculosis and was left laid up in bed for weeks.

Motown reissued 'My Guy' in 1972 and it hit the number fourteen spot in the UK charts, earning her a surprise appearance on the popular live music show *Top Of The Pops*. Some two years later, riding high on the memories of her past musical successes, Mary Wells quit the music industry to take care of her family. Unfortunately her personal life was nothing short of tragic for a woman who deserved so much better. She married Bobby Womack's brother Cecil in 1966 and had three children but their marriage broke up in 1977.

A disastrous secret affair followed with another Womack brother, Curtis, which resulted in Mary taking an overdose as public knowledge exposed the couple's relationship leaving Mary to lose herself in a cocaine and heroin addiction. More heartbreak followed in 1992 when Mary was given the news that her cancer had returned, and it eventually claimed her life on July 26th 1992. She was only forty-nine years old, raising the question of what could have been if only she had lived longer. Mary Wells was cremated and laid to rest in the Womack family crypt in Glendales Forest Lawn Memorial Park Los Angeles.

Mary Wells was awarded a Pioneer Award by the Rhythm and Blues Foundation followed by a Grammy Award for 'My Guy', and inducted into the Hall of Fame in 1999. The Foundation actually raised over fifty thousand dollars to help her pay for urgent ongoing medical treatment after her fight against the cancer had left her penniless. In 2006 she was inducted into the Michigan Rock and Roll Legends Hall of Fame and in 2017 was nominated twice into the Rock and Roll Hall of Fame, but that accolade is yet to awarded; so please, I implore you, isn't it about time that you got your fingers out and recognised one of the true great ladies of Tamla Motown? You all spent many a happy hour singing and dancing along to 'My Guy'.

GLADYS KNIGHT

A true legend of soul music with or without Motown, Gladys Knight was born in Atlanta Georgia to father Merald Woodrow Knight and mother Sarah Elizabeth following one sister and two brothers. Early proof of her talent came when she won a television amateur hour show at the tender age of only seven years old. Encouraged by her success, Gladys formed the Pips with her family members, and they worked with a number of record labels before scoring their first hit single 'Every Beat Of My Heart', recorded on the Vee Jay label. A second single followed on the Fury label, 'Letter Full Of Tears', backed up by their first album. In 1966 they joined Motown, although there was a feeling that Gordy looked on them as an inferior act that might not have the potential to go all the way. Gladys and her Pips were made of strong stuff, and they were able and determined to show everyone that they were going to become successful.

Among their early big hits was a version of 'I Heard It Through The Grapevine', 'Take Me In Your Arms And Love Me', 'Friendship Train', 'I Don't Want To Do Wrong' and 'Neither One Of Us Wants To Be The First To Say Goodbye'. The latter single earned them their first Grammy Award. Impressed by their success, Gordy sent them on tour as the opening act for Diana Ross and the Supremes, but for

Gladys and her Pips, the tour was unexpectedly cut short. The reason was that they out performed Diana Ross; and when the news got back to Gordy he wouldn't stand for anybody messing up his number one act. Gladys took her Pips and signed a lucrative deal with Buddah Records in 1973, where she made Gordy really think twice about his decision to let her go. The single 'Midnight Train To Georgia' was a massive global hit, taking the number one spot on both the R and B and Pop charts as well as earning the group a second Grammy Award. Soon more instantly recognisable, internationally successful Gladys Knight And The Pips hits followed, such as 'I've Got To Use My Imagination', 'The Way We Were', and 'You're The Best Thing That Ever Happened To Me'.

Around the same time as her music was becoming successful, Gladys decided to change direction, starring in a not so successful movie called *Pipe Dreams*. It was a romance set in the Alaskan outback that failed badly at the box office, but on the flip side, Gladys emerged from the wreckage by being awarded a Golden Globe nomination for best new actress. After a number of legal troubles appeared on the horizon regarding ownership of her songs, the Pips split up briefly, allowing her to record a new solo album under the name Miss Gladys Knight before reuniting the Pips in 1980. They finally parted company in 1987.

Then in 1991 Gladys recorded what was to become her most successful album, *Good Woman*, which claimed the number one spot on the R and B album chart and forty-five on the *Billboard* chart. This was the precursor to her enjoying a successful varied musical and film career as an actress as well as recording movie theme tunes. Some two years later her thirtieth album *Where My Heart Belongs* hit number forty in the R and B chart. Both with the Pips and in her solo career, Gladys Knight amassed an awesome number of awards for her outstanding contribution to the music industry including seven Grammys, Best Pop and R and B vocal group, The 1992 Essence Award for Achievement, The Hollywood Walk of Fame in 1995, A Lifetime Achievement Award in 2005, The NAACP Award For Outstanding Jazz Artists, the 2007 Society of Singers Award, and the 2011 Soul Train Music Lifetime Achievement Award. The one and only Gladys Knight - who was once described as "The Empress Of Soul".

THE CONTOURS

The Contours were a male group once described as easily the wild bunch of Tamla Motown, with Berry Gordy warning others to “stay away from those cats because they’re hoodlums”. They were formed in 1960 by five original members - although the line up changed over the years - Billy Hoggs, Billy Gordon, Joe Billingslea, Leroy Fair and Hubert Johnson. They originally called themselves The Blenders. Their musical break came when a local recording studio owner Wes Higgins offered them an audition, but nothing really came of it apart from Higgins liking one of their tracks despite him not liking the group.

Once again fate stepped in after spotting the name of the Higgins record label and deciding to rename the group the Contours and the rest is history, as it was with so many potential young stars searching for that unique something that would help get them noticed enough by Berry Gordy to give them a contract. After an audition in Hitsville showcasing their rough but potential talent, Gordy decided he liked them, but despite this, sent them packing to get their act together and come back in six months when they were ready. Hubert Johnson, whose cousin was none other than Jackie Wilson, agreed to listen to what they had to offer and was so impressed he spoke to Gordy telling him that he was sure he’d found a new group called the Contours who were destined to go places, with a little work.

After a second audition in Hitsville, they signed a seven year recording contract with Motown, but their first single ‘Whole Lotta Woman’ crashed and burned without trace. Gordy was a man who placed great importance on not only a group's vocal style but also their dancing style, meaning that because Leroy Fair couldn't dance to save his life, his Motown career ended as quickly as it began. He was replaced briefly by Martha Reeves's brother Ronnie, and then by Sylvester Potts, and Gordy released their second single, a new version of 'Whole Lotta Woman' that once again crashed and burned; so it was down to Motown's A and R man, Mickey Stephenson, to make a success of the Contours before they were politely shown to the door never to return to Hitsville again.

Clearly the guys had potential; but their next single, 'The Stretch', also did nothing. It was time for Berry Gordy to intervene, informing them that he had written a song originally penned for the Temptations who were nowhere to be seen at the time. With their Motown career reaching the do or die stage, Gordy gave them 'Do You Love Me' to work on and add their own magic touch to, and that's what the Contours did. Gordy was impressed enough to release it in September 1962, and it worked. The single stormed into the charts, claiming the number three spot on the Pop chart and an incredible number one on the R and B chart.

The Contours had pulled off the impossible in their hour of need, earning them a place on the ill-fated Tamla Motown UK Soul Revue, during which they are given the chance to record an album *Do You Love Me Now I Can Dance,* which reached numbers forty-two and twenty-one on the Pop and R and B charts respectively. More success followed in 1964 with their single 'Can You Do It', written and produced by Motown's in house quality control man Richard Street; the single hit number sixteen on the *Cashbox* R and B chart and forty-one on the pop chart. However, despite their growing success, The Contours were far from happy with Motown, preferring to spend more time touring as it was better paid as opposed to studio recording work. In the end four of them decided to call it a day, leaving original member Billy Gordon all alone and out on a precarious limb. With a string of new and old members coming and going, work began on some material with Smokey Robinson and one of his Miracles, Bobby Rogers, producing a new single which was released in 1965. It was called 'First I Look At The Purse' and it reached number twelve on the R and B chart and a lowly fifty-seven on the Pop chart. The song provided successful cover material in the years to come and was performed by the J Giles Band, David Bromberg and Rod Stewart.

The Contours continued to record a wealth of new unreleased material, ready and waiting for future generations to enjoy. At the end of their contract with Motown, in 1968, they left, but two years later Gordy saw fit to release their biggest UK hit single, 'Just A Little Misunderstanding'. It was yet another Motown monster that became a massive anthem on the UK northern soul scene thanks once again to Ian Levine's Motor City Records, who also released the CD compilation *Best Of The Contours*. Their musical legacy continues thanks to the efforts of UK based Kent Records, which released two CD compilations including rare material recorded in Hitsville, and in 2015 the Contours were inducted into the R and B Hall of Fame and rightly so. From the second 'Just A Little Misunderstanding' begins to pick up the beat, it's an invitation to the dancefloor, and it's impossible to refuse the temptation of a leisurely shuffle, singing and clapping in time to one of the greatest soul records ever released; it's clear irrefutable evidence of a time when the Contours were absolutely without doubt on top of their game.

THE FOUR TOPS

The Four Tops comprised of Levi Stubbs, Renaldo "Obie" Benson, Lawrence Peyton and Abdul "Duke" Fakir, four young guys with big dreams who began their musical career in 1954 performing as a harmony group in and around the Detroit area. Following some unsuccessful recordings with record labels Chess Columbia and Riverside they finally found the label that was going to change their lives forever. After signing for Tamla Motown in April 1963 they were put to work alongside Holland Dozier Holland who presented them with 'Baby I Need Your Loving', and as a result the Four Tops well and truly arrived. The record was a top twenty hit and was the first in a series of similar hits with backing and vocals provided by the Funk Brothers and the Andantes. 'The Same Old Song', 'Something About You', and 'Shake Me Wake Me' led to what is for me their signature song, forever synonymous with the Four Tops, 'Reach Out I'll Be There'. This was released in 1966 and was greeted with global acclaim. It was followed by two more successful singles, 'Standing In The Shadows Of Love' and the haunting 'Bernadette'.

Their live shows put the Four Tops on a whole new level of both respect and success, as Brian Epstein promoted them for their first tour of the UK with their main single

'Walk Away Renee', which was taken from the album *Reach Out*, oblivious to the fact that they were about to face a sudden shocking change in their careers when Holland Dozier Holland quit Motown. The Four Tops decided to head off in a fresh new experimental direction, letting their strong harmonies take the lead as they teamed up with the Supremes on a chart hit 'River Deep Mountain High'. They went on to record three albums.

The Four Tops quit Motown in 1972 with Renaldo Benson collaborating with Marvin Gaye on his album *What's Going On,* after which their popularity began to waiver for a number of years. Then in 1983 Motown called them up asking if they would like to appear on a television show celebrating the label's twenty-fifth anniversary alongside the Temptations. Together they put on a show that wowed the audience who had grown up on their music, signalling several sell out tours as well as a successful run on Broadway. Like a prodigal son returning home for some much needed tender loving care after being in the desert for too long, the Four Tops once again signed for Motown in 1983, recording their album appropriately titled *Back Where I Belong*, followed by a second one, *Magic*, and a brilliant appearance on the Live Aid stage.

In the hugely successful Hollywood movie *Little Shop Of Horrors*, the voice of the carnivorous plant is that of Levi Stubbs, and the film went on to be nominated for an Oscar, giving him the chance to perform the song live at the Academy Awards ceremony. In 1998 he performed another film lead song, 'Loco In Acapulco', which was originally penned by Holland Dozier Holland and reached the UK Top Ten chart.

In 1997 the Four Tops' long term successful musical partnership came to a sad end with the death of Lawrence Peyton. As recognition for their immense contribution to the music industry, in 2009 the Four Tops were honoured with a Grammy Lifetime Achievement Award. The Four Tops were without doubt one of the greatest groups to come out of the Hitsville factory.

THE TEMPTATIONS

Of course you cannot mention the Four Tops without including their musical partners in crime the Temptations, definitely one of Motown's most successful male groups of all time, who started out their musical career as two different groups before joining together as one. The original members comprised of Eddie Kendricks, who later went on to enjoy a successful solo career, Paul Williams, Otis Williams, Melvin Franklyn and Eldride "Al" Bryant who called themselves the Temptations. Their first single, 'Dream Come True' produced by Gordy, only managed to make the lower echelons of the R and B chart. Their third single, though, 'My Girl', exploded into the *Billboard* Hot 100, claiming the number one spot, and was written by the one and only Smokey Robinson. With Al Bryant replaced by David Ruffin, their future success was signed, sealed and delivered. A succession of big hits followed: 'Get Ready', 'Ain't Too Proud To Beg', 'I Know I'm Losing You' and 'I Wish It Would Rain' backed up by four successful albums, *Wish It Would Rain, In A Mellow Mood, Getting Ready* and *With A Hot Soul*.

Enter Norman Whitfield, who decided to take the Temptations off into a brand new and different Motown style direction. David Ruffin was sacked for allowing his annoying ego to get the better of him on one too many occasions and the band introduced the new singer, Dennis Edwards, whose voice was so much more suited to what Whitfield had in mind for the group. A top ten single called 'Cloud Nine' was followed by 'Runaway Child Running Wild' and the instantly recognisable 'I Can't Get Next To You', giving the Temptations a second number one, and their classic reflection on the rapidly changing world, 'Ball of Confusion'.

They joined the Supremes to feature on an album of duets as Eddie Kendricks dropped out of the group because he couldn't reach the high falsetto notes. Norman Whitfield joined forces with friend and fellow songwriter Barrett Strong and together they handed the Temptations a Grammy Award for their 1972 single 'Papa Was A Rolling Stone' behind 'Cloud Nine'. It was Motown's first ever single to earn the label a Grammy. After a spell at Atlantic records, they returned to the fold, joined by old friends Eddie Kendricks and David Ruffin, appearing with their old rivals the Four Tops on a television spectacular celebrating the twenty-fifth anniversary of Tamla Motown. It was a performance so good that the two groups joined together on a mammoth tour lasting some four years.

The Temptations are still recording and performing after an amazing thirty-seven top forty singles, four of which were number one singles; on the R and B charts they had fifteen number one singles and seventeen number one albums. They have enjoyed a sensational and lasting career in the music industry, mixed in with some sadness along the way. After hitting an emotional low point in his life, one of the original founder members, Paul Williams, hit the booze, suffering intense depression after he was diagnosed with sickle cell anaemia. Unable to keep up with the intense pressures of touring, he left the group, planning to record a number of solo projects that never came to fruition. On the

17th August 1973, in a Detroit back alley, Paul was found dead in his car with an empty bottle of booze by his side. The cause of death was suicide with no suspicious circumstances despite being found with two gunshot wounds to the head and if that isn't suspicious then I don't know what is. They leave a rich musical legacy to say the least: 1965 Grammy Award nomination for Best R and B Recording for 'My Girl', 1968 Grammy Award Winners for Best R and B Performance by a Vocal Group for 'Cloud Nine', 1972 Grammy Award Winners for Best R and B Performance by a Vocal Group for 'Papa Was A Rolling Stone', 1998 Grammy Award nomination for Best R and B Performance for 'Stay', Best Traditional R and B Performance for the album *Phoenix Rising,* 2000 Grammy Award winners for Best Traditional R and B Album for *Ear Resistible*, 2002 Grammy Award nomination for Best R and B Vocal Performance for 'Lady', 2006 Grammy Award winners for Best Traditional R and B Vocal Performance for 'How Sweet It Is Top Be Loved By You', 2013 Grammy Award Lifetime Achievement Award – and that's not bad going at all.

R DEAN TAYLOR

Canadian born songwriter and producer R Dean Taylor was a rarity within the Motown hierarchy, a white guy in a black stable, and he was responsible for one of my lasting favourite Motown songs, 'There's A Ghost In My House' - with a typical driving beat, thumping bass lines, drum rolls and great vocals, what is there not to like? Born in 1939 in Toronto, R Dean began his musical career writing a succession of singles that ended up playing on both local and national radio and television programmes. A friend of Berry Gordy managed to secure him an audition in Hitsville, and after spending some creative time with Brian Holland and Lamont Dozier he was offered a contract as a staff writer and quickly began adding his own stamp on many of their songs.

R Dean soon found himself thrown into the thick of things and in 1965 Motown released his first single, called 'Let's Go Somewhere', but this failed to hit the intended mark. Undaunted, he found himself working with and contributing to songs written by Norman Whitfield and engineer Frank Wilson for established artists like the Four Tops, the Temptations, Brenda Holloway, the Marvelettes and Gladys Knight and the Pips. In 1967 Motown released another R Dean single called 'There's A Ghost In My

House', an instantly recognisable classic Motown sound that did little in the US but claimed the number three spot in the UK charts; it became his signature single, alongside 'I Gotta See Jane'. His success continued and he penned 'I'll Turn To Stone' and 'All I Need' for the Four Tops and the Temptations, as well as a string of future hits for Diana Ross and the Supremes, following the unexpected and unthinkable departure of the legendary Holland Dozier Holland.

Sensing that a change in direction for Tamla Motown was well overdue, Berry Gordy created a label within a label called Rare Earth, featuring a number of white artists who R Dean was assigned to work with. His first single for the new label, called 'Indiana Wants Me', turned out to be a huge success, reaching the number one spot in Canada and number five on the *Billboard* Hot 100. Future releases proved less successful and eventually Rare Earth was wrapped up in 1976. R Dean Taylor, the man who was once recognised as being the most underrated act to have ever recorded with Tamla Motown, and I for one totally agree.

THE ISLEY BROTHERS

The Isley Brothers were formed in the 1950s by three brothers – Rudolph, Ronald and Vernon O'Kelly, cutting their musical teeth like so many young artists in gospel music, before Vernon was tragically killed in a motorcycle accident. Shortly after moving to New York the two brothers found themselves recording for a number of labels, releasing two singles, 'Shout' and 'Twist And Shout', which the Beatles covered, reaching number seventeen in the Hot 100 and number two in the R and B charts, which they held for an incredible nineteen weeks. During this time The Isleys also formed their own record label, T Neck Records, attracting the attention of none other than Jimi Hendrix, who played guitar on two singles – 'Testify' and 'Move On Over And Let Me Dance'. Both singles crashed and burned, failing to reach the charts, so sadly Jimi packed up his guitar said goodbye and moved on to more favourable climes.

Their first Motown single, released in 1966, called 'This Old Heart Of Mine', oozes all the classic early qualities of the time and became a big enough hit to convince Gordy to record an album that not only showcased their music but also featured some great covers from Marvin Gaye, Martha Reeves and the Vandellas and the Supremes. Their second single, 'I Guess I'll Always Love You', also proved to be a hit and was successful both in the US and the UK.

Striking while the iron was hot, Motown released a second album, *Soul On The Rocks*, featuring two of their greatest hit singles – ‘Behind A Painted Smile’ and the massively popular, one hundred miles an hour ‘Tell Me It’s Just A Rumour’, which became synonymous with the Isley Brothers forever. Due to their massive success in the UK they decided to pack up and move to England for a time to take stock as well as capitalising on their success. The Isley Brothers left Tamla Motown in 1968 and continued pursuing their musical careers with different line ups. They were inducted into the R and B Hall of Fame in 1992 followed by the Vocal Group Hall of Fame in 2003 and they have left their handprints on Hollywood’s Walk of Fame forever: a worthy testament to a group who brought so much happiness to all of us who were into soul music back in the day.

EDWIN STARR

In the Motown family there were artists and there were showman artists who went the extra mile to perform above and beyond their talent and give their audiences a night they would remember forever - and Edwin Starr was one such showman artist. He was born Charles Edwin Hatcher on the 21st January 1942 in Nashville and was the creator of his first group in 1957. Going under the name of the Future Tones, he recorded for Ric Tic Records after moving to Detroit, scoring a big success in 1965 with his single 'Agent OO Soul', which set the standard for all Edwin Starr recordings to come. This was followed by more hits - 'Headline News', 'Backstreet' and 'SOS Stop Her On Sight'. Sensing there was going to be some stiff competition to deal with from Ric Tic Records, Berry Gordy stepped in and bought the company before closing it down and signing Edwin to Motown.

Edwin's first Motown release was an album called *Soul* featuring a compilation of his old classic Ric Tic material plus a selection of established Motown covers. His biggest single success was '25 Miles', along with the controversial 'War', written by Barrett Strong and Norman Whitfield, a personal reaction to the three years he served in the US military in Vietnam, thankful to return home in one piece when so many didn't. Edwin built up a massive faithful following on the UK northern soul scene, so much so that he left the US to live in the UK permanently, where his live shows were the stuff of dreams.

Edwin Starr died aged sixty-one in 2003 in Nottingham, with a gravestone that sums up the love the northern soul scene had for him that reads "Our Agent OO Soul." Edwin tuned up to a jam-packed Wigan Casino in the 70s and put on a show the likes of which I've never seen again. For over two solid sweat-soaked hours he delivered his catalogue of hits in true showmanship style, visibly stunned by the faithful crowd that matched his every lyric word for word. Many times throughout the show we were so loud that we drowned him out, leaving him simply standing there in wonderment, pointing the microphone to the audience and silently taking in the unforgettable soulful vibe created by all those present on that wonderful night.

MARVIN GAYE

I think I can safely say with total assurance that most of us during our lives have days - be they good, bad or indifferent - that we'll remember forever, whether it's being in a special place with good friends or mourning the death of a family member. For me I couldn't believe the news circulating around the world on the 1st April 1984 that one of Tamla Motown's greatest voices (many say the greatest, but as with beauty that lies with the beholder) was shot dead by his own father during a bitter family feud, trying to protect his mother. Pronounced dead by the time he arrived at the California Hospital Medical Centre, just one day short of his forty-fifth birthday, of course I'm talking about the late great Marvin Gaye, cut down in the prime of his ever maturing artistic talent, whose tragic premature death left an unfillable void in the Motown family.

Marvin was born on April 2nd 1939, his father a church minister and his mother a domestic. The family lived in a housing project called the Fairfax Apartments like many others that were springing up across America back in the day. These projects were the government's nasty solution to providing predominantly black people with cheap, badly constructed housing, and many were massively overcrowded and even lacking essential everyday services like water and electricity. Eventually many were demolished and replaced by modern housing while others remained to become violent drug dealing no-go ghettos where even angels and policemen feared to tread, offering no hope to those desperate to escape to a better, safer life.

Marvin had two sisters and two brothers and his childhood was nothing short of brutal and terrifying; he was regularly subjected to vicious beatings from his father and he once described his life as like living with a changeable, cruel and all-powerful king. He suffered untold abuse well into his teenage years and freely admitted that he seriously contemplated suicide countless times and would have done so were it not for the continued support of his brothers and sisters. After a brief time in the US air force he was given a discharge and returned to civilian life to begin an early musical career as a singer songwriter.

His love of the doo-wop sound saw the young Marvin forming a group called the Marquees. During this time he was fortunate enough to come into contact with a man called Harvey Fugua, who became his lifelong mentor and closest friend. Fugua invited Marvin to join his own group the Moonglows and as a result of Fugua's friendship with Berry Gordy, Marvin was called into Hitsville to allow Gordy to assess whatever potential he had that was worth investing in. Despite the failure of his first album, *The Soulful Moods Of Marvin Gaye*, Gordy already knew he had the talent for greatness and put him to work with Smokey Robinson, recording a series of songs that all hit various positions both in the R and B and Pop charts thanks to singles like 'Can I Get A Witness', 'How Sweet It Is', 'I'll Be Doggone' and 'Ain't That Peculiar'. These singles, alongside hit duets with Kim Weston, Mary Wells and Tammi Terrell, more than justify his presence within the Motown hierarchy.

But the success of all those releases paled into insignificance when a song penned by Norman Whitfield catapulted Marvin into superstardom. His heavenly soulful voice added a magic spirituality to the song he made his own. 'I Heard It Through The Grapevine' was released in 1968 and became Motown's greatest hit of the decade, hitting the number one spot on the charts for some seven weeks. Marvin's truly distinctive voice, singing Whitfield's excellent lyrics and with the Funk Brothers' outstanding backing created an almost out of body experience that people the world over tuned into. I mean, how many of us haven't heard it through the grapevine that the girl we thought we were in love with has gone off with a new love at least one time in our lives?

Marvin Gaye was never a Motown artist to simply lie down and allow Gordy to stroke his belly whenever he wanted to. The more he matured the more he became a constant thorn in his boss's side, especially during the 70s when his music echoed the feelings he harboured deep inside telling him to follow his inner voices and that now was the time to change. His brother was serving in Vietnam, fighting a pointless war America was never going to win as more and more soldiers returned home in body bags. The Peace Movement was gaining massive support as violent anti-war demonstrations became a daily occurrence on university campuses throughout America, urging fellow Americans to burn their draft cards and refuse to fight.

With a voice sent down from heaven, Marvin Gaye's vocals on his classic album *What's Going On*, claimed by many to be the greatest album ever recorded, asks the question that is still waiting to be answered in the world today, reflecting the social and racial troubles raging across the modern world. Two more albums followed, attracting a huge following of women and understandably so with the titles 'Let's Get It On' and 'I Want You', much to

Berry Gordy's strong disapproval. Struggling with a big cocaine addiction and the IRS chasing him for unpaid taxes, Marvin packed up and headed for Belgium, where he lived in an apartment in Ostend in a determined bid to clean his life up, turning to a local church to help him do this.

With rumours that he was planning a musical comeback, as well as a final break from Tamla Motown, CBS records were prompted to sign him and he began work on a new album, released in September 1982, called *Midnight Love.* That kicked off a US tour and a year later at the NBA's All Star game in LA, he performed a brilliant emotional rendition of the US national anthem accompanied by deafening silence and a flood of tears. The album featured the lead single 'Sexual Healing' which became his biggest ever hit; and all from a modest apartment in Belgium. It reached number seven on the Hot Black Singles Chart, becoming the biggest hit of the 1980s, attaining massive international success and selling over two million copies. The single won Marvin his first two Grammy Awards including one for Best Male R and B Vocal Performance in February 1983. *People* magazine called it the biggest musical sexual turn on since Olivia Newton John told us all to 'Get Physical' as it reached number one on the Black Albums Chart selling over six million copies worldwide.

Marvin Gaye was cremated at Forest Lawns Memorial Park in LA and his ashes were scattered in the Pacific Ocean. His father, Marvin Gaye Senior, was arrested and charged with first degree murder, later reduced to voluntary manslaughter after doctors detected a brain tumour. Because of this he was given a six year suspended jail sentence and died in a nursing home in 1998.

It would be a far easier task to list the awards Marvin Gaye didn't receive for his outstanding service to the music industry. He was inducted into the Rock and Roll Hall of Fame in 1987, followed by his own star on the Hollywood

Walk of Fame in 1990. In 1996 he was posthumously awarded a Grammy Lifetime Achievement Award. The Rock and Roll Hall of Fame listed 'I Heard It Through The Grapevine', 'What's Going On' and 'Sexual Healing' in their top 500 list of songs that shaped the face of rock and roll.

Rolling Stone magazine ranked him number eighteen on their list of one hundred greatest artists of all time, sixth on their list of one hundred greatest singers of all time and eighty-two on their list of one hundred greatest songwriters of all time. *Q* magazine ranked him sixth on their list of one hundred greatest singers. Three of his albums - *What's Going On*, *Let's Get It On* and *Here My Dear* - were ranked by *Rolling Stone* on their list of the five hundred best albums of all time - *What's Going On* was at number six on the *Rolling Stone* list and actually topped the *New Musical Express* top one hundred albums of all time.

In 2003 he was included by the Library of Congress in its National Recording Registry. Four of his songs - 'I Heard It Through The Grapevine', 'What's Going On', 'Let's Get It On' and 'Sexual Healing' - made it on to the *Rolling Stone* list of the five hundred greatest songs of all time. In 2005 he was inducted into the Michigan Rock and Roll Legends Hall of Fame. In 2014 he was inducted into the official Rhythm and Blues Hall of Fame in its second class. In 2016 he was posthumously inducted into the Songwriters Hall of Fame. In 2008 Marvin Gaye's estate earned some three and half million dollars, earning him the macabre accolade of taking thirteenth place in the list of top earning dead celebrities. Unlucky for some, particularly so for Marvin Gaye, one of the greatest soul artists of all time.

DAVID RUFFIN

Respected by all for his brilliant, effortless singing voice, the former Temptations vocalist, who had left them to pursue a solo career, was tragically found dead after an overdose in 1991 at the age of fifty, after enjoying a lengthy tour in the UK. His family firmly believe his death was a result of foul play. His final moments were surrounded by poverty, so much so that Michael Jackson stepped up to the frame and paid for all his funeral expenses.

David Ruffin was born in 1941 in Whynot, close to the town of Meridian in Mississippi, the son of Baptist minister Elias Ruffin and mother Ophelia Ruffin. His father's religious influence rubbed off on young David, who began his musical career in the family gospel group before spreading his wings after suffering an abusive, frequently violent childhood. The newly emerging soul sound of Sam Cooke and Jackie Wilson was a huge influence on him, so he decided to change his direction and jump on board the new soul train about to sweep across America. He met Berry Gordy, and if the rumours are true, he rolled up his sleeves and helped him build Hitsville, although Berry Gordy's first wife Raynona might have a different version of things.

During this time he met Marvin Gaye, who tried him out and was so impressed with the young man's voice that he invited him to join the Temptations in 1964. He immediately stamped his individuality on three of their early big hits, 'My Girl', 'Ain't To Proud To Beg' and 'I Know I'm Losing You'. He was however forced out of the Temptations because of his increasingly troublesome behaviour.

He had solo success. His brother joined him on his second album, *I Am My Brother's Keeper*, which featured the forever classic 'Stand By Me', which reached the UK charts as well as other places in Europe.

His finest album is considered to be *Taken*, which wasn't released until 2004, after his death, and really it is a joy to listen to, full of slices of soul and funk at their best, aided and abetted by the legendary Funk Brothers. The single 'Taken', from the album, was also a hit. He was a brilliant artist who promised so much more, who was plagued by demons that finally got the better of him and quite possibly took root in him when he was a child. A singer fondly remembered by Martha Reeves, who said "nobody can sing like David Ruffin". In 2019 the city of Detroit honoured him by naming a street " The David Ruffin Street" for his contribution to music.

EDDIE KENDRICKS

Another of my favourite Motown stars, Eddie Kendricks enjoyed a successful career both with the Temptations and solo in the time he was at Tamla Motown. Born in Union Springs on the 17th December 1939 to Johnny and Lee Bell Kendrick with one sister and three brothers, it was in the church choir in Birmingham where he met a young man he would go on to share to so much success with, Paul Williams, one of the future Temptations. They formed a group called the Cavaliers and began playing in and around the Birmingham area, where they met Milton Jenkins, who offered to manage them. Acting on his suggestion of moving to Detroit, they renamed themselves the Primes and were soon proving popular with their audiences. Eventually they teamed up with an all-girl group called the Primettes, who would eventually become the Supremes, and so the early embryo of the Temptations began to grow.

As well as his truly unique singing voice Eddie also had ideas about the how the Temptations would look on stage, having some sharp purple suits made up for each member to match their even sharper dance moves, but sadly the suits were only worn the one time, never to be seen again. Eddie featured on many of the early classic Temptations hits as Norman Whitfield began to steer them away from the tried and tested romantic ballads into the strange world of psychedelic soul. It was a sound that Eddie wanted no part of, and a sound that eventually caused him to leave the Temptations, as the tensions between the band gradually worsened. He left Motown in 1978, and during a television interview his only comment when asked about Berry Gordy was "I don't know the man. I only met him three times but I know he didn't particularly care for me."

After spells with Arista and Atlantic Records his career was on a downward slope, due to damage he was doing to his throat as a result of the number of cigarettes he was getting through. Teaming up with the Temptations occasionally, and planning to record and tour with his old friend David Ruffin, fate dealt them both the cruellest of hands. David Ruffin died of an overdose in 1991 and Eddie Kendricks was diagnosed with throat cancer. Despite having one lung removed, he returned to touring, but time was running out for him. Admitted to a hospital in Birmingham, Eddie died on October 5th 1992, aged fifty-two years old. Having left a long and varied catalogue of singles and albums behind him, he won many awards with the Temptations, and on October 16th 1999, the Eddie Kendricks Memorial Park in Birmingham was created. There's a fitting memorial in the form of a bronze statue of the man himself as well as sculptures of the Temptations beside him. In 2019 he was inducted as a solo artist into the National Rhythm and Blues Hall of Fame, a much deserved honour for one of the greatest Tamla Motown stars.

FRANK WILSON

Out of all the myths and legends that have surrounded Tamla Motown over the decades, the story behind Frank Wilson is my favourite. Born in Houston on December 5th to James Wilson and Samantha Gibbs, he was a person passionate about civil rights. While he was a student at Southern University in Baton Rouge, his participation in a civil rights demonstration cost him his scholarship, so he ended up in Los Angeles searching for a new direction and he found one when Motown producer Hal Davis offered him a job in Motown´s Los Angeles office.

It soon became clear that he had more than a good feel for song writing when he helped to produce Patrice Holloway's single 'Stevie', after which Frank received the call from Berry Gordy offering him a job in Hitsville. Naturally he jumped at the chance and soon found himself in the thick of things working alongside Marvin Gaye, the Supremes, Brenda Holloway, the Four Tops and the Temptations and others. Following the shock departure of Holland Dozier Holland, Frank's role at Motown became vitally important in continuing to produce the songs; but Frank was a man of many talents, both inside and outside Motown. He launched his own record companies - Traco Music and Specolite Music - through which he published, recorded and released over forty songs before one particular song propelled him into musical history.

In 1965 Frank found himself back in Hitsville on the new secondary label Motown Soul producing a song called 'Do I Love You (Indeed I Do)', a record that was full of what the classic Motown sound is all about. According to legend there were only two hundred and fifty copies pressed, with only five copies surviving, making it the world's rarest, most valuable soul single of all time, and one copy sold in 2009 for over twenty-five thousand pounds. After years of helping to produce a stable of Motown songs, Frank quit the music industry to concentrate on becoming a minister, travelling around the world to spread the good word. He died of cancer in 2012 aged seventy-one, leaving his wife Bunny and five children.

Frank Wilson's 1965 single has once again come under the spotlight in 2020, when a young millionaire from the UK paid what is reported to be one hundred thousand pounds for the privilege of owning the world's rarest Tamla Motown single.

STEVIE WONDER

Can you possibly imagine you are eleven years old and blind when you are given the chance to sign for Tamla Motown? Well that's exactly what happened to "Little" Stevie Wonder, who went on to become one of Motown's greatest artists ever. Two years later, in 1963, his first single 'Fingertips' defied all the odds by claiming the number one spot on the *Billboard* Hot 100 chart, and he was only thirteen years old, making him the youngest artist to ever take the number one spot.

Stevie Wonder's birth name was Stevland Hardaway Judkins, and he was born in Saginaw on May 13th 1950 to mother Lula Maye Hardaway and father Calvin Judkins. Fate dealt the infant a vicious cruel blow as he went blind almost from birth as a result of being born premature and exposed to oxygen rich air in the incubator. His parents divorced, after which his mother moved to Detroit with her six children, where Stevie displayed a talent for singing in the church choir at the Whitestone Baptist church. Despite his crippling disability he also began playing a variety of musical instruments, particularly the piano and harmonica, which would become his trademark instruments later on in his career. At eleven years old he performed one of his early songs called 'Lonely Boy' to none other than Ronnie White of the Miracles, who was so impressed with the youngster's talent that he convinced Berry Gordy to give him an audition, after which a recording contract followed. The deal included a five year contract in which all his royalties would remain in a secure trust fund until he reached his twenty-first birthday. Until that time Gordy made sure he received a weekly sum enough for him and his mother to live on.

He recorded a Berry Gordy song called 'I Call It Pretty Music But The Old People Call It The Blues' which stormed to the top of the *Billboard* Hot 100 chart, giving him his second number one. An unexpected setback followed in the wake of his success, as his voice changed as he was growing up - and not for the better - to the point that Motown actually discussed cancelling his contract, but the young Stevie Wonder dug his heels in. No longer going by the nickname of "Little Stevie", he overcame his vocal problems before a series of successful singles were released. 'Uptight', 'I Was Made To Love Her' and 'For Once In My Life' were nicely balanced out with some textbook Stevie Wonder harmonica solos, and later followed by the two classics 'Superstition' and 'Living For The City'.

Stevie Wonder beat all imaginable odds facing him to become a world class superstar, though for many Motown fans, it was his early music, produced in the recording studio of Hitsville USA Detroit, that they hold dearest to their heart. Two of his later albums, *Inner Visions* and *Songs In The Key Of Life*, remain two of the greatest, most influential albums of all time and he is responsible for recording over thirty US top ten hits, including ten number ones, and selling over one hundred million records His many and varied music awards include him being nominated as one of the top sixty best selling artists of all time, and winning an incredible twenty-five Grammy Awards, including a Lifetime Achievement Award. He was inducted into the Rock and Roll Hall of Fame and the Rock and Roll

Songwriters Hall of Fame and has his own star on the Hollywood Walk of Fame. He was inducted into the Rhythm and Blues Hall of Fame and *Rolling Stone* magazine named him as the greatest singer of all time. Not too bad an achievement for a young kid born blind with an ambition to play music. Hats off to Mister Stevie Wonder.

BEHIND THE PAINTED SMILE

Back in 1994 I couldn't wait to get my hands on a copy of the book I'd been dying to read ever since I heard about its publication date. The title was called *To Be Loved - The Music - The Magic - The Memories of Motown* - it was the long-awaited autobiography from Mister Motown himself, Berry Gordy. It was a hugely personal account from the creator of Motown, all about the number of budding stars who walked through the doors of Hitsville hoping and praying for their big break, some leaving broken-hearted if they just didn't have that rare special magic on the day to make it, while others who delivered a great audition in Studio A signed the recording contract that would change their lives forever.

Being a lifelong Motown fan of course I was going to read the pages slowly, so as to not miss a single detail, like sipping on a fine bottle of wine, as I turned the pages enjoying the story of the man who'd given me so many unforgettable memories over the years with good friends along the way. I mean, there was no way I was going to be disappointed as I stretched out on the bed and started my journey. Right from the beginning Gordy buckles you in and takes you on his incredible journey from childhood to creating Motown. Night after night he was scouring the nightlife in Detroit searching for potential talent he could turn into superstars. Just as he ran Motown virtually singlehandedly, this characteristic is present in much of his story, told in enough colourful prose to put you off swearing forever.

The story hits home right from the beginning that he was a man in the right place at the right time, with a dream, fully determined and unafraid to take chances to make that dream a success. He was very much the business man, at the head of a different factory but a factory all the same, churning out black American soul records instead of chicken wings. He touches on his family, where his journey began, where he came from and his family roots with honesty; as he does later on in the book about his vices, money, music, gambling and women. His recollections as to how the artists came together and sang songs tailored to meet their vocal styles was for me reminiscent of walking into a tailor's shop to get measured up for a bespoke suit. To read how the music that I bought and danced to was made was brilliant, especially the early Detroit Motown that for me was the best musical period. I particularly enjoyed the early part of the story and how he tracked down potential he instantly knew that he could turn into successful artists and global names like Diana Ross, Smokey Robinson, Marvin Gaye, Michael Jackson and so many more. The relationships he managed to build with them, like they were all one big family, were fascinating. They were an immensely talented dysfunctional family who became friends, lovers and often enemies. And then of course the sad parts followed, when it came to artists who'd been with Motown since it began leaving the fold for whatever personal reasons they had, often financial ones; but that was a common problem with the recording industry back in the day. I also got the feeling that if he'd have pulled his foot off the gas more than he did, and given his artists more freedom to do their own thing, then perhaps Tamla Motown would still be producing records.

I found the early part of his story the most fascinating, and I enjoyed not knowing what to expect with each new page. As to the rest of it, I felt it to be rather light on detail as to the real story of what went on behind the doors of Hitsville any night of the week. Surely you don't get a man like Gordy hanging around with that number of musicians and singers, some of whom had come from the roughest parts of Detroit, without indulging in the kind of wild, messed up parties I used to wake up from, nursing a hangover from hell, when the question I would ask as I turned to the lovely stranger lying in the bed next to me was "Where the hell am I and what's your name love?" I mean, there is Gordy, freely airing his vices and yet choosing to ignore what surely must have played a part in Motown. Many artists grew up in the housing projects where drugs became a way of life and there is no shame in admitting this. After all, how many great paintings, books, music and films have been created under the influence of drugs (*Apocalypse Now* just one that springs to mind)? Surely, to my way of thinking, this must have been the case when everybody was doing their bit in Studio A.

To all those who walked through the doors of Hitsville, Gordy offered the chance of untold fame and fortune, even down to the art of grooming them for the public eye he knew would be watching their every move. What Gordy didn't offer was a private health care plan for those who fell by the wayside. Marvin Gaye struggled with a heavy cocaine addiction for decades as a result of the constant abuse he suffered at the hands of a violent father. Bass player James Jamerson died a broken alcoholic. Temptations member Paul Williams committed suicide and David Ruffin died after a drug overdose. Two ladies of Motown ended their lives in abject poverty, Mary Wells eventually succumbing to throat cancer and Supremes singer Florence Ballard dying from a massive heart thrombosis. Sufficient enough proof that being a part of the Motown hierarchy did not always end up with the fame and fortune they dreamed about.

And the burning question, a suggestion that quite a few people have confirmed and the one that he vehemently denies, is whether he had any dealings with the Detroit mafia when he needed cash to keep Tamla Motown in business. It was also clear from the book that Gordy had his own inner circle of Tamla superstars, who feature quite a lot in the story, but for me he could have included more lesser known Motown artists to add some more flavour to the book. Much to my surprise I only read it the one time and left it with mixed feelings. Was Gordy's lengthy story the truth, the whole truth and nothing but or was he wearing cautious, rose-tinted shades when he wrote the book in order to protect his public image?

It was an intriguing question I'd never find the answer to - or so I thought, until I read a book called *Berry, Motown and Me* written by his former wife Raynona Gordy Singleton, published four years before Gordy's. I read the book twice and found it to be a heart-breaking, emotional, sad and frequently disturbing account of what really went on behind the scenes in Hitsville, or at least what really went on according to Raynona Gordy Singleton. It was a story that couldn't have been more different to Gordy's, told by a person who was not only there but who played an integral part in establishing the early Motown set up, offering strong evidence to the old adage that there are most definitely two sides to every story. It's a story that is littered with anger, pain, sadness and disappointment.

A woman who was recognised as an accomplished musician, songwriter, and producer in her own right, she tells her story of how it was behind the closed doors of

Hitsville. The inspiration for Tamla Motown, who received no recognition from Gordy despite the fact that she was the joint founder member of the label, she claims that she found the property that became Hitsville as well as creating the iconic sign that was fixed to the building. Detroit born and bred, her first love was classical music, playing in orchestras, where she developed the skills to play eleven instruments. She had a natural beautiful voice that helped her to develop many young Motown artists' talents to their full potential, and she also wrote and arranged music. One quality of her book is that you can really feel that all she wanted with Gordy was true love and romance but that was never going to be enough for him, a self-confessed womaniser who had strings of women chasing him in downtown Detroit.

When things between them started to become nasty, Gordy had her shipped out to run Motown's publishing company Jobette in New York after she pulled a gun on the new woman in Gordy's life. She claims that in New York she had absolutely no money whatsoever to live on. With no other choice she went to the trouble of pressing up some singles of 'My Guy' that she sold behind Gordy's back. It was a move that got her arrested by the FBI, but in order to save her from going to prison, Gordy didn't press charges, mainly because she had a child of his, who would have gone into a care home or to foster parents.

During the many times the label was short of cash in order to survive, Raynona says that she had no option other than to become a prostitute to make ends meet, and all in all her story makes for shocking reading. When the book was published Gordy was incensed that his squeaky clean public image was tarnished, so to save maximum embarrassment he went to the trouble of purchasing as many copies as possible so that people could not read her book. In view of Gordy creating what became the greatest recording label in history, cash flow was always going to be problem in the early days, but reading what Raynona recalls of those days is quite heart-breaking if all of it is true. She was even ignored, as if she didn't exist, at the grand twenty-fifth anniversary of Motown celebration; she was just a person in the crowd, watching from the balcony.

Years later Gordy claimed that she had retracted much of what she had said about him in the book and that they were now "closer than ever." Miss Ray simply spoke of her relationship with Gordy with the following words: "He's got all the money but he didn't end up with the appearance that he wanted. That perfect person who helps Boy Scouts. I could have continued to protect his name but I would have been a martyr." After all the animosity between them over the years, things seemed to end on a much happier understanding, Gordy mentioning Miss Ray in his book and admitting that she had actually withdrawn some of the accusations she'd made about him and that they were closer than ever as well as giving her some long overdue personal credit for playing a big part in the early development of Tamla Motown, which he'd remained silent about for decades. On November 11th 2016 Miss Ray died at the age of seventy-nine.

After reading Raynona's moving story, I still loved Motown music - it was the main music I listened to as a teenager, impatiently waiting for each week to pass knowing that the record shop would be stocked up on all the latest releases - but the fact remains that Berry Gordy treated her badly enough for her to need to write her story. It was, I thought, a true insight into Hitsville that I might never have known about. As the Motown dream began to gather momentum with next to no money, if Raynona hadn't been by his side, helping to keep the dream alive the way she did, Motown may well have died an early death.

In my opinion, Berry Gordy, despite his faults, would have succeeded in anything he chose to do business wise. If he had continued with his boxing, then he would have been world champion. If he'd chosen to stay in the military he would have reached the rank of general and if he'd have stayed on the automotive production line he would have ended up owning the company. He was just that kind of guy. He was fearless in taking on new business ideas and had a rare talent for spotting potential superstars. Jimmy Webb, who was the chairman of the Rock and Roll Hall of Fame, spoke about his incredible lifetime achievement as follows: "Berry Gordy is an innovator and visionary. He created a label but more than that he created a genre. He pioneered a market place for Afro American artistry and then he invited the world in to enjoy it. Berry was ahead of his time. His young immaculately groomed artists were the first in the world to receive media training. Berry Gordy and the Motown sound are essential to the American music story."

He produced seventy-nine records in the *Billboard* Hot 100, and was inducted into the Rock and Roll Hall of Fame in 1988. In 2011 President Obama staged a salute to Motown in the grounds of the White House, and in 2013 he was awarded a legacy in motion lifetime award. In 2016 he was awarded a National Medal of Arts. He wrote and co-wrote over two hundred songs in the Motown catalogue, and in his work with the Civil Rights Movement, he edited and released an album containing many of the original speeches by Doctor Martin Luther King, which made up for the many accusations that his political stance and work within Motown did not support the Civil Rights Movement enough. He produced two films, *Lady Sings The Blues* and *Mahogany* starring Diana Ross, his true lifelong obsession in the leading roles of both films. Tamla Motown provided the background music for sixty years of world change: the space race, JFK and Martin Luther King assassinations, Civil Rights and the Peace Movement, race riots in the deep south, hippies and Woodstock, the Apollo space programme and the man on the moon, the Berlin Wall knocked down, the advent of computers and mobile phones, the Internet, Google and Apple giving people instant access of information at the touch of a finger, the first African American Barack Obama taking the White House, the fight against Islam, Saddam Hussein toppled, the Twin Towers.

Not too shabby for a young black guy arriving in Detroit with only eight hundred dollars in his pocket and a dream of starting what would evolve into the most successful black American soul music label of all time. Sixty years of Motown have gone in the click of a finger, and if I could tell him anything, I'd say thanks very much for giving me and all my friends so many great memories since I first got bitten by the Motown bug. It was the sound that changed America as well as helping to create a music scene in the UK that is still going strong over fifty years later. From John O' Groats to Lands End there will be a soul night going on somewhere, playing some early Motown classics, if you know where to look. Some years ago while I was deejaying at Lancaster University I had some six hundred singles stolen, including many original labels that I have never been able to replace; but the memories - they are something that will stay with me forever. It's been a hell of a ride but one I would not have missed for the world. Happy Birthday Tamla Motown.

45 Discography for Motown Records

Motown	1000	The Satintones	Sugar Daddy My Beloved	Feb-1960
Motown	1001	Eugene Remus	You Never Miss A Good Thing Gotta Have Your Lovin'	Mar-1960
Motown	1001	Eugene Remus	You Never Miss A Good Thing Hold Me Tight	Mar-1960
Motown	1002	Popcorn and The Mohawks	Custer's Last Man Shimmy Gully	Jun-1960
Motown	1003	Mary Wells	Bye Bye Baby Please Forgive Me	Dec-1960

Motown	1004	Sherri Taylor and Singin' Sammy Ward	Oh Lover	Sep-1960
			That's Why I Love You So Much	
Motown	1005	Henry Lumpkin	I've Got A Notion	Jan-1961
			We Really Love Each Other	
Motown	1006	The Satintones	Tomorrow And Always	Mar-1961
			A Love That Can Never Be	1st issue
Motown	1006	The Satintones	Angel	Apr-1961
			A Love That Can Never Be	2nd issue
Motown	1007	Debbie Dean	Don't Let Him Shop Around	Feb-1961
			A New Girl	
Motown	1008	The Contours	Whole Lotta Woman	Feb-1961
			Come On And Be Mine	
Mot	10	The Supremes	I Want A Guy	Mar-1961
			Never Again	promo only

own	08			
Motown	1009	Richard Wylie and his Band	Money (That's What I Want) I'll Still Be Around	Apr-1961
Motown	1010	The Satintones	I Know How It Feels My Kind Of Love	Jun-1961
Motown	1011	Mary Wells	I Don't Want To Take A Chance I'm So Sorry	Jul-1961 P/S:Y
Motown	1012	The Contours	The Stretch Funny	Jul-1961
Motown	1013	Henry Lumpkin	What Is A Man (Without A Woman) Don't Leave Me	Jan-1962
Motown	1014	Debbie Dean	Itsy Bity Pity Love But I'm Afraid	Aug-1961

Motown	1015	The Golden Harmoneers	I Am Bound Precious Memories	Aug-1961
Motown	1016	Mary Wells	Strange Love Come To Me	Sep-1961 P/S:Y
Motown	1017		[not issued]	
Motown	1019	Popcorn and The Mohawks	Real Good Lovin' Have I The Right	Oct-1961
Motown	1020	The Satintones	Zing Went The Strings Of My Heart Faded Letter	Oct-1961
Motown	1021	Eddie Holland	Jamie Take A Chance On Me	Oct-1961
Mot	10	Twistin' Kings	Xmas Twist	Nov-1961

own	22		White House Twist	
Motown	1023	Twistin' Kings	Congo - Part 1 Congo - Part 2	Dec-1961
Motown	1024	Mary Wells	The One Who Really Loves You I'm Gonna Stay	Feb-1962 P/S:Y
Motown	1025	Debbie Dean	Everybody's Talkin' About My Baby I Cried All Night	Mar-1962 P/S:Y
Motown	1026	Eddie Holland	You Deserve What You Get Last Night I Had A Vision	Apr-1962
Motown	1027	The Supremes	(He's) Seventeen Your Heart Belongs To Me	May-1962 P/S:Y
Motown	1028	Herman Griffin	Sleep (Little One) Uptight	Jun-1962

Motown	1029	Henry Lumpkin and The Lovetones	Mo Jo Hanna Break Down And Sing	Jul-1962
Motown	1030	Eddie Holland	If Cleopatra Took A Chance What About Me	May-1962 P/S:Y
Motown	1031	Eddie Holland	If It's Love (It's Alright) It's Not Too Late	Aug-1962
Motown	1032	Mary Wells and The Lovetones	You Beat Me To The Punch Old Love (Let's Try It Again)	Aug-1962 P/S:Y
Motown	1033	La Brenda Ben and the Vandellas	Camel Walk The Chaperone	Oct-1962
Motown	1034	The Supremes	Let Me Go The Right Way Time Changes Things	Nov-1962
Mot	10	Mary Wells	Two Lovers Operator	Oct-1962

own	35			
Motown	1036	Eddie Holland	Darling I Hum Our Song Just A Few More Days	Dec-1962
Motown	1037	Linda Griner	Good-By Cruel Love Envious	Feb-1963
Motown	1037	Linda Griner	Good-By Cruel World Envious	Feb-1963
Motown	1038	Amos Milburn	I'll Make It Up To You Somehow My Baby Gave Me Another Chance	Feb-1963
Motown	1039	Mary Wells	Laughing Boy Two Wrongs Don't Make A Right	Feb-1963
Motown	1040	The Supremes	My Heart Can't Take It No More You Bring Back Memories	Mar-1963

Motown	1041	Connie Van Dyke	Oh Freddie It Hurt Me Too	Mar-1963
Motown	1042	Mary Wells	Your Old Stand By What Love Has Joined Together	May-1963
Motown	1043	Eddie Holland	Brenda Baby Shake	Jun-1963
Motown	1044	The Supremes	A Breath Taking, First Sight Soul Shaking, One Night... (The Man With The) Rock And Roll Banjo Band	Jun-1963 1st issue
Motown	1044	The Supremes	A Breath Taking Guy (The Man With The) Rock And Roll Banjo Band	Jun-1963 2nd issue
Motown	1045	Holland-Dozier	What Goes Up - Must Come Down Come On Home	Aug-1963

Motown	1046	Amos Milburn	My Daily Prayer I'll Make It Up To You Somehow	Jul-1963
Motown	1046	The Serenaders	If Your Heart Says Yes I'll Cry Tomorrow	Jul-1963
Motown	1046	The Skyliners	Since I Fell For You I'd Die	1963 test press only
Motown	1047	Morrocco Muzik Makers	Back To School Again Pig Knuckles	Sep-1963
Motown	1048	Mary Wells	You Lost The Sweetest Boy What's Easy For Two Is So Hard For One	Aug-1963
Motown	1049	Eddie Holland	I'm On The Outside Looking In I Couldn't Cry If I Wanted To	Oct-1963
Mot	10	Carolyn Crawford	Forget About Me Devil In His Heart	Oct-1963

own	50			
Motown	1051	The Supremes	When The Love Light Starts Shining Through His Eyes Standing At The Crossroads Of Love	Nov-1963
Motown	1052	Eddie Holland	Leaving Here Brenda	Dec-1963
Motown	1053	Bobby Breen	How Can We Tell Him Better Late Than Never	Jan-1964
Motown	1054	The Supremes	Run, Run, Run I'm Giving You Your Freedom	Feb-1964
Motown	1055	Sammy Turner	Only You Right Now	Mar-1964
Moto	1056	Mary Wells	My Guy	Mar-1964

wn			Oh Little Boy (What Did You Do To Me)	
Motown	1057	Marvin Gaye and Mary Wells	Once Upon A Time What's The Matter With You Baby	Apr-1964 P/S:Y
Motown	1058	Eddie Holland	Just Ain't Enough Love Last Night I Had A Vision	May-1964
Motown	1059	Bobby Breen	You're Just Like You Here Comes That Heartache	May-1964
Motown	1060	The Supremes	Where Did Our Love Go He Means The World To Me	Jun-1964 P/S:Y
Motown	1061	Mary Wells	When I'm Gone Guarantee (For A Lifetime)	Jul-1964
Motown	1062	The Four Tops	Baby I Need Your Loving Call On Me	Jul-1964

Motown	1063	Eddie Holland	Candy To Me If You Don't Want My Love	Aug-1964
Motown	1064	Carolyn Crawford	My Smile Is Just A Frown Turned Upside Down I'll Come Running	Aug-1964 1st issue
Motown	1064	Carolyn Crawford	My Smile Is Just A Frown (Turned Upside Down) I'll Come Running	1964 2nd issue
Motown	1065	Mary Wells	Whisper You Love Me Boy I'll Be Available	not issued
Motown	1066	The Supremes	Baby Love Ask Any Girl	Sep-1964 P/S:Y
Motown	1067	The Spinners	Sweet Thing How Can I	Oct-1964
Mot	10	The Supremes	Come See About Me	Oct-1964

own	68		Always In My Heart	
Motown	1069	The Four Tops	Without The One You Love (Life's Not Worthwhile) Love Has Gone	Nov-1964
Motown	1070	Carolyn Crawford	My Heart When Someone's Good To You	Dec-1964
Motown	1071	Tony Martin	Our Rhapsody Talkin' To Your Picture	Dec-1964
Motown	1072	Choker Campbell's Big Band	Come See About Me Pride And Joy	Dec-1964
Motown	1073	The Four Tops	Ask The Lonely Where Did You Go	Jan-1965 P/S:Y
Motown	1074	The Supremes	Stop! In The Name Of Love I'm In Love Again	Feb-1965 P/S:Y

Motown	1075	The Supremes	Back In My Arms Again Whisper You Love Me Boy	Apr-1965 P/S:Y
Motown	1076	The Four Tops	I Can't Help Myself (Sugar Pie, Honey Bunch) Sad Souvenirs	Apr-1965
Motown	1077	Billy Eckstine	Had You Been Around Down To Earth	May-1965
Motown	1078	The Spinners	I'll Always Love You Tomorrow May Never Come	Jun-1965
Motown	1079	The Supremes George Alexander and The Supremes	The Only Time I'm Happy Supremes' Interview .	Jun-1965
Motown	1080	The Supremes	Nothing But Heartaches He Holds His Own	Jul-1965 P/S:Y
Mot	10	The Four Tops	Its The Same Old Song	Jul-1965

own	81		Your Love Is Amazing	
Motown	1082	Tony Martin	The Bigger Your Heart Is (The Harder You'll Fall) The Two Of Us	Aug-1965
Motown	1083	The Supremes	I Hear A Symphony Who Could Ever Doubt My Love	Oct-1965
Motown	1084	The Four Tops	Something About You Darling, I Hum Our Song	Oct-1965
Motown	1085	The Supremes	Children's Christmas Song Twinkle, Twinkle Little Me	Dec-1965 P/S:Y
Motown	1086	Tammi Terrell	I Can't Believe You Love Me Hold Me, Oh My Darling	Dec-1965
Motown	1087	Barbara Mc Nair	Touch Of Time You're Gonna Love My Baby	Dec-1965

Motown	1088	Tony Martin	Ask Any Man Spanish Rose	Jan-1966
Motown	1089	The Supremes	My World Is Empty Without You Everything Is Good About You	Dec-1965
Motown	1090	The Four Tops	Shake Me, Wake Me (When It's Over) Just As Long As You Need Me	Feb-1966
Motown	1091	Billy Eckstine	Slender Thread Wish You Were Here	Mar-1966
Motown	1092	Connie Haines	What's Easy For Two Is So Hard For One Walk In Silence	Apr-1966
Motown	1093	The Spinners	Truly Yours Where Is That Girl	Apr-1966
Mot	10	The Supremes	Love Is Like An Itching In My Heart	Apr-1966

own	94		He's All I Got	
Motown	1095	Tammi Terrell	Come On And See Me	May-1966
			Baby Don'tcha Worry	
Motown	1096	The Four Tops	Loving You Is Sweeter Than Ever	May-1966
			I Like Everything About You	
Motown	1097	The Supremes	You Can't Hurry Love	Jul-1966
			Put Yourself In My Place	P/S:Y
Motown	1098	The Four Tops	Reach Out I'll Be There	Aug-1966
			Until You Love Someone	P/S:Y
Motown	1099	Barbara Mc Nair	What A Day	Sep-1966
			Everything Is Good About You	
Motown	1100	Billy Eckstine	A Warmer World	Sep-1966
			And There You Were	

Motown	1101	The Supremes	You Keep Me Hangin' On	Oct-1966
			Remove This Doubt	P/S:Y
Motown	1102	The Four Tops	Standing In The Shadows Of Love	Nov-1966
			Since You've Been Gone	
Motown	1103	The Supremes	Love Is Here And Now You're Gone	Jan-1967
			There's No Stopping Us Now	
Motown	1104	The Four Tops	Bernadette	Feb-1967
			I Got A Feeling	
Motown	1105	Billy Eckstine	I Wonder Why (Nobody Loves Me)	Feb-1967
			I've Been Blessed	
Motown	1106	Barbara Mc Nair	Here I Am Baby	Mar-1967
			My World Is Empty Without You	
Mot	11	The Supremes	The Happening	Mar-1967

own	07		All I Know About You	
Motown	1108	Paul Peterson	Chained Don't Let It Happen To You	Apr-1967
Motown	1109	The Spinners	For All We Know Cross My Heart	Apr-1967
Motown	1110	The Four Tops	Seven Rooms Of Gloom I'll Turn To Stone	May-1967
Motown	1111	Diana Ross and The Supremes	Reflections Going Down For The Third Time	Jul-1967
Motown	1112	Barbara Mc Nair	Steal Away Tonight For Once In My Life	Jul-1967
Motown	1113	The Four Tops	You Keep Running Away If You Don't Want My Love	Aug-1967

Motown	1114	Chris Clark	From Head To Toe The Beginning Of The End	Sep-1967
Motown	1115	Tammi Terrell	What A Good Man He Is There Are Things	Oct-1967
Motown	1116	Diana Ross and The Supremes	In And Out Of Love I Guess I'll Always Love You	Oct-1967
Motown	1117	The Ones	You Haven't Seen My Love Happy Day	Nov-1967
Motown	1118	Chuck Jackson	(You Can't Let The Boy Overpower) The Man In You Girls Girls Girls	Jan-1968
Motown	1119	The Four Tops	Walk Away Renee Your Love Is Wonderful	Jan-1968
Mot	11	Billy Eckstine	Is Anyone Here Going My Way	Jan-1968

own	20		Thank You Love	
Motown	1121	Chris Clark	Whisper You Love Me Boy The Beginning Of The End	Feb-1968
Motown	1122	Diana Ross and The Supremes	Forever Came Today Time Changes Things	Mar-1968
Motown	1123	Barbara Mc Nair	Where Would I Be Without You For Once In My Life	Mar-1968
Motown	1124	The Four Tops	If I Were A Carpenter Wonderful Baby	Apr-1968
Motown	1125	Diana Ross and The Supremes	What The World Needs Now Is Love Your Kiss Of Fire	not issued
Motown	1126	Diana Ross and The Supremes	Some Things You Never Get Used To You've Been So Wonderful To Me	May-1968

Motown	1127	The Four Tops	For Once In My Life Yesterday's Dreams	Jun-1968
Motown	1128	Marvin Gaye Gladys Knight and The Pips	His Eye Is On The Sparrow Just A Closer Walk With Thee .	Jun-1968
Motown	1129	Paul Peterson	A Little Bit For Sandy Your Love's Got Me Burnin' Alive	Aug-1968
Motown	1130	The Ones	Don't Let Me Lose This Dream I've Been Good To You	Aug-1968
Motown	1131	Billy Eckstine	For Love Of Ivy A Woman	Sep-1968
Motown	1132	The Four Tops	I'm In A Different World Remember When	Sep-1968
Mot	11	Barbara Mc Nair	You Could Never Love Him (Like I Love Him)	Sep-1968

own	33		Fancy Passes	
Motown	1133	Barbara Mc Nair	You Could Never Love Him (Like I Love Him) You Could Never Love Him (Like I Love Him)	Sep-1968 promo
Motown	1134	Blinky	I Wouldn't Change The Man He Is I'll Always Love You	Oct-1968
Motown	1135	Diana Ross and The Supremes	Love Child Will This Be The Day	Sep-1968
Motown	1136	The Spinners	I Just Can't Help But Feel The Pain Bad, Bad Weather (Till You Come Home)	Nov-1968
Motown	1137	Diana Ross and The Supremes and The Temptations	I'm Going To Make You Love Me A Place In The Sun	Nov-1968 P/S:Y
Moto	1138	Tammi Terrell	This Old Heart Of Mine (Is Weak For You)	Dec-1968

wn			Just Too Much To Hope For	
Motown	1139	Diana Ross and The Supremes	I'm Living In Shame I'm So Glad I Got Somebody (Like You Around)	Jan-1969
Motown	1140	David Ruffin	My Whole World Ended (The Moment You Left Me) I've Got To Find Myself A Brand New Baby	Feb-1969
Motown	1141	Soupy Sales	Muck-Arty Park Green Grow The Lilacs	Feb-1969
Motown	1142	Diana Ross and The Supremes and The Temptations	The Way You Do The Things You Do I'll Try Something New	Feb-1969
Motown	1143	Billy Eckstine	My Cup Runneth Over Ask The Lonely	Mar-1969
Moto	1144	Chuck Jackson	Are You Lonely For Me Baby Your Wonderful Love	Apr-1969

wn				
Motown	1145	Jonah Jones	For Better Or Worse Don't Mess With Bill	not issued
Motown	1146	Diana Ross and The Supremes	The Composer The Beginning Of The End	Mar-1969
Motown	1147	The Four Tops	What Is A Man Don't Bring Back Memories	Apr-1969
Motown	1148	Diana Ross and The Supremes	No Matter What Sign You Are The Young Folks	Jun-1969
Motown	1149	David Ruffin	I've Lost Everything I've Ever Loved We'll Have A Good Thing Going On	Jul-1969
Motown	1150	Diana Ross and The Supremes and The Temptations	Stubborn Kind Of Fellow Try It Baby	Aug-1969

Motown	1151	Captain Zap and The Motortown Cut-Ups	The Luney Take-Off The Luney Landing	Jul-1969
Motown	1152	Chuck Jackson	Honey Come Back What Am I Gonna Do Without You	Sep-1969
Motown	1153	Diana Ross and The Supremes and The Temptations	The Weight For Better Or Worse	Sep-1969
Motown	1154	Joe Harnell	Midnight Cowboy Green Grow The Lilacs	Sep-1969
Motown	1155	The Spinners	In My Diary (She's Gonna Love Me) At Sundown	Sep-1969
Motown	1156	Diana Ross and The Supremes	Someday We'll Be Together He's My Sunny Boy	Oct-1969
Mot	11	The Jackson 5	I Want You Back Who's Lovin' You	Oct-1969

own	57			
Motown	1158	David Ruffin	I'm So Glad I Fell For You I Pray Every Day You Won't Regret Loving Me	Dec-1969
Motown	1159	The Four Tops	Don't Let Him Take Your Love From Me Don't Let Him Take Your Love From Me	Nov-1969 promo
Motown	1159	The Four Tops	Don't Let Him Take Your Love From Me The Key	Nov-1969
Motown	1160	Chuck Jackson	The Day My World Stood Still Baby, I'll Get It	Dec-1969
Motown	1161	Joe Harnell	My Cheri Amour Green Grow The Lilacs	Jan-1970
Moto	1162	The Supremes	Bill, When Are You Coming Home	Feb-1970

wn			Up The Ladder To The Roof	
Motown	1163	The Jackson 5	ABC	Feb-1970
			The Young Folks	P/S:Y
Motown	1164	The Four Tops	It's All In The Game	Mar-1970
			Love (Is The Answer)	P/S:Y
Motown	1165	Diana Ross	Reach Out And Touch (Somebody's Hand)	Apr-1970
			Dark Side Of The World	P/S:Y
Motown	1166	The Jackson 5	I Found That Girl	May-1970
			I Found That Girl	
Motown	1166	The Jackson 5	I Found That Girl	May-1970
			The Love You Save	
Motown	1166	The Jackson Five	The Love You Save	May-1970
			The Love You Save	

Motown	1167	The Supremes	Everybody's Got The Right To Love	Jul-1970
			But I Love You More	
Motown	1168	Blinky	How You Gonna Keep It (After You Get It)	Jul-1970
			This Time Last Summer	
Motown	1169	Diana Ross	Ain't No Mountain High Enough	Jul-1970
			Can't It Wait Until Tomorrow	P/S:Y
Motown	1170	The Four Tops	Still Water (Love)	Aug-1970
			Still Water (Peace)	
Motown	1171	The Jackson 5	I'll Be There	Aug-1970
			I'll Be There	promo
Motown	1171	The Jackson 5	I'll Be There	Aug-1970
			One More Chance	
Mot	11	The Supremes	Stoned Love	Oct-1970
			Shine On Me	

own	72			
Motown	1173	The Supremes and The Four Tops	River Deep, Mountain High Together We Can Make Such Sweet Music	Nov-1970
Motown	1174	The Jackson 5	Santa Claus Is Coming To Town Christmas Won't Be The Same This Year	Nov-1970
Motown	1175	The Four Tops	Just Seven Numbers (Can Straighten Out My Life) I Wish I Were Your Mirror	Dec-1970 P/S:Y
Motown	1176	Diana Ross	Remember Me What About You	Dec-1971 P/S:Y
Motown	1178	David Ruffin	Don't Stop Loving Me Each Days Is A Lifetime	Feb-1971
Moto	1179	The Jackson 5	Never Can Say Good-Bye She's Good	Mar-1971

wn				
Motown	1180	Gordon Staples and The Motown Strings	Strung Out Sounds Of The Zodiac	Apr-1971
Motown	1181	The Supremes and The Four Tops	You Gotta Have Love In Your Heart I'm Glad About It	May-1971
Motown	1182	The Supremes	Nathan Jones Happy (Is A Bumpy Road)	Apr-1971
Motown	1183	Bobby Darin	Melodie Someday We'll Be Together	Apr-1971
Motown	1184	Diana Ross	Reach Out I'll Be There (They Long To Be) Close To You	Apr-1971
Motown	1185	The Four Tops	In These Changing Times Right Before My Eyes	May-1971

Motown	1186	The Jackson 5	I Will Find A Way Maybe Tomorrow	Jun-1971
Motown	1187	David Ruffin	You Can Come Right Back To Me Dinah	Jul-1971
Motown	1188	Diana Ross	Surrender I'm A Winner	Jul-1971
Motown	1189	The Four Tops	MacArthur Park - Part 1 MacArthur Park - Part 2	Aug-1971
Motown	1190	The Supremes	Touch Its So Hard For Me To Say Goodbye	Sep-1971
Motown	1191	Michael Jackson	Got To Be There Maria (You Were The Only One)	Oct-1971
Mot	11	Diana Ross	I'm Still Waiting	Oct-1971

own	92		A Simple Thing Like Cry	
Motown	1193	Bobby Darin	Simple Song Of Freedom I'll Be Your Baby Tonight	Nov-1971
Motown	1194	The Jackson 5	Sugar Daddy I'm So Happy	Nov-1971
Motown	1195	The Supremes	Floy Joy This Is The Story	Dec-1971
Motown	1196	The Four Tops	A Simple Game L.A. (My Town)	Jan-1972
Motown	1197	Michael Jackson	Rockin' Robin Love Is Here And Now You're Gone	Feb-1972
Motown	1198	The Four Tops	I Can't Quit Your Love Happy (Is A Bumpy Road)	Apr-1972

Motown	1199	The Jackson 5	Little Bitty Pretty One If I Have To Move A Mountain	Apr-1972
Motown	1200	The Supremes	Automatically Sunshine Precious Little Things	Apr-1972
Motown	1201	Jermaine Jackson	That's How Love Goes I Lost My Love In The Big City	Aug-1972
Motown	1202	Michael Jackson	I Wanna Be Where You Are We've Got A Good Thing Going	May-1972 P/S:Y
Motown	1203	Bobby Darin	Sail Away Something In Her Love	May-1972
Motown	1204	David Ruffin	A Little More Trust A Day In The Life Of A Working Man	Jun-1972
Mot	12	The Jackson 5	Looking Through The Windows	Jun-1972

own	05		Love Song	
Motown	1206	The Supremes	Your Wonderful, Sweet Sweet Love	Jul-1972
			The Wisdom Of Time	
Motown	1207	Michael Jackson	Ben	Jul-1972
			You Can Cry On My Shoulder	
Motown	1208	The Naturals	Good Things (Where Was I When Love Came By)	Jul-1972
			Me And My Brother	
Motown	1209	Jerry Ross Symposium	Duck You Sucker	Sep-1972
			It Happened On A Sunday Morning	
Motown	1210	The Four Tops	(It's The Way) Nature Planned It	Aug-1972
			I'll Never Change	
Moto	1211	Diana Ross	Good Morning Heartache	Dec-1972
			God Bless The Child	P/S:Y

wn				
Motown	1212	Bobby Darin	Average People Something In Her Love	Sep-1972
Motown	1213	The Supremes	I Guess I'll Miss The Man Over And Over	Oct-1972
Motown	1214	The Jackson 5	The Corner Of The Sky To Know	Oct-1972
Motown	1215	Jerry Ross Symposium	Take It Out On Me It's The Same Old Love	Nov-1972
Motown	1216	Jermaine Jackson	Daddy's Home Take Me In Your Arms (Rock Me A Little While)	Nov-1972
Motown	1217	Bobby Darin	Happy (Love Theme From "Lady Sings The Blues") Something In Her Love	Nov-1972

Motown	**1218**	**Michael Jackson**	**With A Child's Heart** **Morning Glow**	**Apr-1973**
Motown	**1219**	**Michel Legrand** **Gil Askey**	**Love Theme From "Lady Sings The Blues"** **Any Happy Home**	**Mar-1973**
Motown	**1220**	**Gil Askey Orchestra**	**Don't Explain** **C.C. Rider**	**Mar-1973**
Motown	**1221**	**Irene "Granny" Ryan**	**No Time At All** **Time (To Believe In Each Other)**	**Apr-1973**
Motown	**1222**	**Willie Hutch**	**Brother's Gonna Work It Out** **I Choose You**	**May-1973**
Motown	**1223**	**David Ruffin**	**Blood Donors Needed (Give All You Can)** **Go On With Your Bad Self**	**Apr-1973**
Mot	**12**	**The Jackson 5**	**You Made Me What I Am**	**Feb-1973**

own	24		Hallelujah Day	
Motown	1225	The Supremes	Bad Weather Oh Be My Love	May-1973
Motown	1226	Vin Cardinal	Shame And Scandal In The Family Never Been To Spain	Jun-1973
Motown	1227	Jermaine Jackson	[not title planned] [no title planned]	not issued
Motown	1228	Reuben Howell	I'll See You Through Help The People	Jun-1973
Motown	1229	Martin and Finley	Thinkin' 'Bout My Baby Best Friends	Mar-1973
Motown	1230	The Jackson 5	Boogie Man Don't Let Your Baby Catch You	Jun-1973

Motown	1231	Irene Ryan	I See Your Name Up In Lights When Yesterday Was Tomorrow	Apr-1973
Motown	1232		[not issued]	
Motown	1233	Blinky	You Get A Tangle In Your Lifeline This Man Of Mine	Mar-1973
Motown	1234	G.C. Cameron	No Matter Where Have I Lost You	Apr-1973
Motown	1235	The Spinners	Together We Can Make Such Sweet Music Bad, Bad Weather (Till You Come Home)	Mar-1973
Motown	1236	Stacie Johnson	Woman In My Eyes Every Little Bit Hurts	Apr-1973
Mo	12	Suzee Ikeda	Time For Me To Go	Apr-1973

town	37		Zip-A-Dee Doo-Dah	
Motown	1238	Celebration	Since I Met	

About the Author

Pete McKenna – author of ten books (five published by NEW HAVEN) on various fiction and non -fiction subjects from music street cultures memoir and crime. Responsible for writing NIGHTSHIFT the first book on the 70´s northern soul scene in and around Wigan Casino as well as a fictonal northern soul crime novel WHO THE HELL´S FRANK WILSON. Interests include reading – film – theatre – military history – travelling – antiques – wining and dining and good friends and the odd dram of single malt.

Lightning Source UK Ltd.
Milton Keynes UK
UKHW011847170321
380525UK00002B/281

9 781912 587353